Social scientists have long been fascinated by the Christian conversion, a form of religious experience that believers say both strengthens their faith and changes their lives. This study looks at the performance of conversion narratives and argues that the performance itself is central to the efficacy of the conversion. Through detailed analysis of a number of conversion narratives, Peter Stromberg shows how these narratives can be understood as a form of ritual, in which believers invoke central emotional conflicts and then attempt to resolve these conflicts by reframing them in terms of the language of Evangelical Christianity. Although the Christian conversion narrative is used as the primary example, the approach in this book also illuminates other practices – such as psychotherapy – in which people deal with emotional conflict through language.

Language and self-transformation

Publications of the Society for Psychological Anthropology 5

Editors
Robert A. Paul, Graduate Institute of the Liberal Arts, Emory University, Atlanta

Richard A. Shweder, Committee on Human Development, The University of Chicago

Publications of the Society for Psychological Anthropology is a joint initiative of Cambridge University Press and the Society for Psychological Anthropology, a unit of the American Anthropological Association. The series has been established to publish books in psychological anthropology and related fields of cognitive anthropology, ethnopsychology and cultural psychology. It includes works of original theory, empirical research, and edited collections that address current issues. The creation of this series reflects a renewed interest among culture theorists in ideas about the self, mind–body interaction, social cognition, mental models, processes of cultural acquisition, motivation and agency, gender and emotion.

1 Roy G. D'Andrade and Claudia Strauss (eds.): *Human motives and cultural models*

2 Nancy R. Rosenberger (ed.): *Japanese sense of self*

3 Theodore Schwartz, Geoffrey M. White and Catherine A. Lutz (eds.): *New directions in psychological anthropology*

4 Barbara Diane Miller (ed.): *Sex and gender hierarchies*

Language and self-transformation

A study of the Christian conversion narrative

Peter G. Stromberg

University of Tulsa, Oklahoma

CAMBRIDGE
UNIVERSITY PRESS

Published by the Press Syndicate of the University of Cambridge
The Pitt Building, Trumpington Street, Cambridge CB2 1RP
40 West 20th Street, New York, NY 10011-4211, USA
10 Stamford Road, Oakleigh, Melbourne 3166, Australia

First published 1993

Printed in Great Britain at the University Press, Cambridge

A catalogue record for this book is available from the British Library

Library of Congress cataloguing in publication data

Stromberg, Peter G.
Language and self-transformation: a study of the Christian
conversion narrative / Peter G. Stromberg.
     p.   cm. – (Publications of the Society for Psychological
Anthropology)
Includes bibliographical references and index.
ISBN 0 521 44077 7 (hard cover)
1. Conversion – Case studies. 2. Language and languages – Religious
aspects – Christianity. I. Title. II. Series.
BR110.S76 1993
248.2′4 – dc20 92-34071 CIP

ISBN 0 521 44077 7 hardback

UP

For my father, Melvin Stromberg

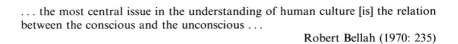

... the most central issue in the understanding of human culture [is] the relation between the conscious and the unconscious ...

Robert Bellah (1970: 235)

Contents

Preface

I am a cultural anthropologist, which means that I am trained first of all to write ethnographies. The reader might reasonably assume, then, that what he or she is preparing to read is an ethnographic study of a group of people who have had "conversion experiences" to Evangelical Christianity. Such an assumption, although reasonable, would be incorrect, and I think it best to be clear about this from the outset. The subject of this study is the dual problem of self-transformation and commitment; those who tell conversion stories generally base those stories in part around the claim that their conversion experiences have changed them in a fundamental way and that these experiences have led to a deepened commitment to their faith. It is these claims that interest me, claims that have ultimately to do with the possibility that a particular language (here, Evangelical Christianity) may bring about self-transformation. Thus I could just as well have studied this process through other languages that make similar claims. (Many religions, for example, claim to be able to bring about self-transformation, as do some secular systems of thought such as certain forms of psychotherapy.) The reader should be forewarned that it is the processes of self-transformation and commitment that are my focus; Evangelical Christianity is the context in which I will observe these processes.

On the argument

I will argue that it is through the use of language in the conversion narrative that the processes of increased commitment and self-transformation take place. This argument is based upon a view of what language is and how it works that is opposed to certain widespread common-sense understandings of these topics. In fact, I will suggest that it is precisely these common-sense understandings of language and subjects (the persons who use language) that set up the conversion narrative by placing some members of our society in a contradictory position. All of this means that I must spend some time talking about common-sense understandings of language in our society and some more time in outlining an alternative view. The first two chapters of the book are devoted to this task. In the first, I introduce a distinction between two forms of communicative behavior, the referential and the constitutive, and argue that common-sense understandings of language tend to assume that all communicative behavior is fundamentally referential. This assumption is associated with a number of other assumptions about minds and persons, and these assumptions are outlined and criticized in the second chapter, entitled "Character and intention."

I begin the third chapter with a brief discussion of my methods of analyzing conversion narratives. It is typical of recent work in social science to attend closely to the actual language in which a story is told, a document is framed, a myth is related, and so on. This work is no exception; it fits into an ever-widening field of inquiry that is often referred to, somewhat ambiguously, as discourse analysis. I devote most of the third chapter to the detailed analysis of a single conversion narrative, that of a woman who seems to have some difficulty in maintaining clear boundaries around herself. By this I mean that, in a number of different contexts – intimate relations, family, work, church membership – this woman has trouble balancing between complete separation from and total merger with her surroundings. It is her use of the language of Christianity that allows her to sustain a balanced connection, as she sees it, to God, and thereby to maintain some balance in her life in general.

The fourth chapter is devoted wholly to the description and analysis of a single conversion narrative, that of a man who engages Christianity explicitly as a therapeutic language to help him come to terms with difficulties in his emotional life. In order to understand his degree of success in this endeavor, I will further develop the distinction between the referential and the constitutive, arguing that self-transformation can occur as a result of shifts between these two forms of communicative behavior. Such shifts have another profound effect as well: as aspects of a religious language come to express previously inarticulable aspects of identity, these aspects come to have profound meaning for believers. This deep sense of meaning is the basis for the other fundamental effect of the conversion narrative, a deepened sense of commitment to the religion.

In chapter 5, entitled "Miracles," I look at the narratives of two believers, a man and a woman, who seem strongly motivated to control various aspects of their lives. Of course, people lack the power to control everything that goes on around them, and ultimately one will have to come to terms, in one way or another, with this fact. The analysis here concerns the ways in which these believers work to come to terms with their largely unacknowledged aim to control through understanding their experience in terms of the language of Evangelical Christianity. To summarize a little too simply, the point is that these believers attribute their unacknowledged aims to God, He who indeed can control all. This resolution is a good example of how the believer can at once come to terms with an emotional ambivalence and strengthen his or her faith by a commitment to the religious language on a very personal and emotional level.

Any oral narrative is acted as well as spoken, and in the chapter entitled "Roles," I turn to two narratives whose dramatic aspects are central to their efficacy. I argue here that as they tell their conversion stories these two believers in essence re-enact both the emotional conflict that led up to the conversion and the resolution of that conflict in terms of the religious language. Such re-enactment can be seen as another example of the relationship between the referential and the constitutive, the ability of the symbol to represent and to constitute ongoing social life. What these believers do is to live out a symbolism that represents a transcendent level, and thus create the possibility of the effective intervention of the transcendent in their lives.

In the conclusion I return to the topic of our society's common sense and its relation to our linguistic ideology. Throughout the book I am concerned with our society's view of the volitional subject, and at the end I will make these concerns more explicit. A brief digression into the topic of psychotherapy will allow me to argue that there are some central contradictions in our common-sense understandings of volition, and that certain social rituals have taken shape as attempts to address and smooth over these contradictions. Indeed, there is a danger that even a social scientist such as myself will be tempted to formulate a ritual solution to these contradictions, probably in the idiom of a theory. I will suggest that any theoretical account of volition is likely merely to appropriate this phenomenon into some powerful theoretical construct such as "the mind" or "language" or "culture." That is, theoretical accounts of volition are more likely to obscure than explain the issue. At the end I will suggest some questions that I regard as more amenable to productive inquiry in social science.

Acknowledgements

In order to do the research on which this book is based, I worked for about a year in a diverse community in California trying to meet, interview, and survey persons who had had conversions. The material on which this book is based came from one part of that study, in which I interviewed, believers I met at an Evangelical church in the community. My first thanks must go to the men and women of that unnamed church who were generous and open in sharing their conversion stories with me. Some of them might feel, if they read this analysis, that I reduce their faith by explaining it in non-spiritual terms, and thereby thank them poorly for their co-operation in this project. I have no idea if it will help, but I would like to remind them – and any believers who read this book – that in focusing on the social and psychological conditions and effects of faith, I make no claims whatsoever about the ultimate validity of that faith.

I would also like to thank the people who supported and facilitated this research. The project was conducted at the Institute of Human Development at the University of California, Berkeley and funded by the National Institute of Mental Health, fellowship number F32 MH08747. Dr Guy E. Swanson of IHD devoted many hours to helping me plan the research, discussing results, and recommending avenues of inquiry. Without him this project could not have been done, and I am very grateful for his help. I have also received timely financial assistance from the research office at the University of Tulsa, both for help in transcribing tapes and for summer money enabling me to devote some much-needed time to writing this book.

A number of colleagues from various disciplines have read portions of this manuscript and offered considerable help through their criticism. Here I would like to thank Tod Sloan, Monty Lindstrom, Herve Varenne, Jim Peacock, Nelly Vanzetti, Steven Laderman, Karen Larsen, Greg Acciaioli, and Niko Besnier. Especially patient and thorough readings of all or part of the manuscript have been provided by Mel Spiro, Susan Chase, John Bowlin, and Steve Leavitt.

Finally I would especially like to thank four persons whose influence has been decisive in determining the course and shape of this work. Jane Hill and Ellen Basso of the Department of Anthropology at the University of Arizona introduced me to the form of analysis I have adopted in this book and provided, through many discussions, many of the basic ideas I am trying to work out here. Robert Paul of the Institute of Liberal Arts at Emory University has been a very supportive series editor, but more importantly, he was the teacher who first introduced me to the possibilities of symbolic and psychological anthropology in my first year of graduate school. It will soon be twenty years since I first encountered Dr. Paul in the classroom, but the problems he brought to my attention at that time remain at the center of my work. Finally, I must thank Ann Swidler (of the Sociology Department of the University of California, Berkeley) once again for her consistent unselfish support and encouragement.

Parts of the second and fifth chapters of this book first appeared in *American Anthropologist* (volume 92, pp. 42–56). Part of the third chapter first appeared in *Ethos* (volume 19, pp. 102–26). These sections appear by permission.

Conventions of transcription

Conventions of transcription (following Moerman 1988, with some modifications; representation of pause length following Varenne n.d.)

{ }   bounds speech spoken softly
{{ }}   bounds speech spoken very softly
CAPS   indicates speech spoken loudly
<u>underlining</u>   indicates words spoken with emphasis
:   extended sound
| | bounds utterances produced simultaneously by two speakers
. . . .   noticeable pause too short to be accurately timed
. . . .   pause of one second. Each dot represents one tenth of a second; thus five dots represents 0.5 second, ten dots 1.0 seconds, thirty-six dots 3.6 seconds, and so on.
(( ))   bounds transcriber's comments
( )   bounds uncertain transcription
'h   soft inbreath
'H   loud inbreath
dec   speech slowing
(ha)   laughter
bounds quickly spoken speech
?   rising intonation
,   falling intonation
=   short transition time
-   preceding sound is cut off

1   Introduction

... and then suddenly as sometimes happens in dreams, out of the corner of my eye again I saw this frieze, a frieze you know that's a stone you know with a . . . sort of three dimensional . . . cut, about twenty to thirty feet high [voice drops to a whisper] and on this frieze there was a picture that was a picture of a combination of Christ on the cross and a Greek athlete. Very powerful, you know what I mean? This wonderful combination of, of the Greek and the Christian. And power, you know I mean I just like it's Christ on the cross but it's not this emasculated . . . this emasculating sort of thing. I'm, I'm putting my own interpretation into the dream now. And I looked at that and it was very interesting because it was very powerful and there were still in the nooks and crannies of this, of this frieze, there was straw, this was something freshly unpacked. And there were bits of straw and bits of tinfoil you know like it hadn't fully come forward yet, that there was still some junk around that I . . . you know, but it was very powerful, the symbol. And then I couldn't stay in the tree any longer, the tree was kind of hollowed out and open, and one – I have a tree in my yard like that – and I found myself coming right out of the tree and with the feeling, 'ah, now I have work to do. I, I have to express this in some way.'

This is a fragment of a narrative I heard in the early 1980s in a city in California. The narrator is a man in his early fifties whom I call Jim; he is telling me about a dream he had had several years earlier, a dream that was significant in the years-long process of his return to the Christianity of his youth.

I had met Jim in the process of conducting participant observation research in a large Evangelical Christian church, and he was the first church member who offered to tell me the story of his "conversion," the experiences that re-established and solidified his Christian faith.[1] I imagine my eyes lit up as I listened to this articulate and psychologically astute man talk for nearly four hours about his "spiritual journey." This was just what I was looking for: an account of the processes whereby a set of widely shared symbols such as "Jesus Christ" and "the cross" came to have intense personal meaning for an individual believer. In grasping the connection between Jim's idiosyncratic personal experience and the language he shares with millions of other believers, I reasoned, I could

1

begin to understand something about the processes whereby a symbolic language such as that of Evangelical Christianity can serve as a link between a believer's deep emotional concerns and a larger community.

The stories that Jim told me fairly bristled with possibilities for this sort of analysis. He had spent years keeping journals, recording his dreams, attending personal growth seminars, and generally ruminating about his past and the possible meanings of what he called "the Christian myth" for his experience. But as I thought about Jim's narrative in the years after I had heard it, as I wrote what seemed like uncountable versions of my analysis of Jim's psychological situation and the part Christianity played in his attempts at personal transformation, I became increasingly aware of a number of problems in my underlying assumptions. Most fundamentally, how did I know that what Jim was telling me was true? This question concerned not Jim's integrity – I assume he made every attempt to co-operate and to tell his story accurately – but rather the much larger issue of the relationship between language and experience (Needham 1972). As Jim had grappled with the problem of understanding his own emotions and experience, he had discovered more or less satisfying ways of labeling that experience and giving it coherence. But this process of meticulously constructing self-understanding required that Jim emphasize some aspects of his experience while downplaying or even excising others, that he replace explanations that had earlier seemed adequate with formulations that now seemed to capture more, in general that he come to see himself in terms of a language that shaped and formed, at the same time as it represented, his experience.

I have now come to doubt my earlier assumption that any language can be assumed to simply re-present experience. I have come to suspect the conviction that behind a subject's language lies a set of events and emotions that the language transparently reflects. I see in this conviction evidence of the power of what I will call the "referential ideology" of meaning in language in American culture (see Silverstein 1979). Americans often assume that language points to an independently existing reality and that it can be used to describe that reality in terms that convey, without fundamentally distorting, its characteristics. Although such an assumption may seem little else than common sense, it is incorrect. The "pointing to a separately existing reality" assumption is wrong in part because language always shapes the reality it describes. But even more important is the fact that the process of referring to events and objects that transcend the actual event of speech is not the sole basis of meaning in language (Hanks 1990: 3). Equally important in the creation of meaning are processes of indexing; language is meaningful to speakers in part because it may reflect a situation beyond the event of speech, but also because it creates a situation in the event of speech (see Duranti and Goodwin 1992 and sources cited there).

In this context the important point is that Jim's conversion narrative is not only or even primarily an account of events from the past, it is a creation of a particular situation in the moment of its telling. The way to look at Jim's conversion, I have come to see, is not as something that occurred in the past and is now "told about" in the conversion narrative. Rather, the conversion narrative itself is a central element of the conversion. The way around the evidential problem I mentioned above is to abandon the search for the reality beyond the convert's speech and to look instead at the speech itself, for it is through language that the conversion occurred in the first place and also through language that the conversion is now re-lived as the convert tells his tale.

On this view it is no coincidence that I encountered a remarkably high level of co-operation as I sought out believers who would be willing to tell me their conversion stories. To do so was, for these believers, not a chore but rather a central ritual of their faith. The conversion narrative offered an opportunity to celebrate and reaffirm the dual effect of the conversion, the strengthening of their faith and the transformation of their lives.[2] This book is an inquiry into this dual process, an attempt to understand both of these effects, and above all an inquiry into the question of why just these two changes should occur together. How does a person's increased commitment to a symbolic system such as Evangelical Christianity also enable him to understand his experience in such a way that his life seems to him to be transformed?

This question has both psychological and sociological dimensions, for to answer it would be to understand something of the therapeutic process in mental health and of the processes of adherence to the groups that are associated with symbol systems. In this book I will not address either of these processes directly, but rather will be content if I can say something quite basic about commitment and the generation of a sense of self-transformation. I will argue that such a sense is closely connected to changes in intentionality in the experience of the narrating subject, changes that are made possible by framing that experience in what I will call a "canonical language" (i.e. a set of symbols concerned with something enduring and beyond everyday reality, such as those associated with "Evangelical Christianity").

One result of this focus is that this is not a book about Evangelical Christianity, although the subjects discussed here profess some version of that faith. I have made no attempt to select a sample of informants that could be said to fairly represent some church or community, nor have I surveyed a broad range of Evangelical churches, for the simple reason that

I do not intend to make any generalizable claims about this religion. Therefore, although I hope that this work will be of some use to the many scholars who are studying conversion, the following is not intended to support claims about conversion in general.[3] My primary concern is rather with how symbol use within a particular tradition can give the actor a sense of self-transformation, and with what these findings might say about how self-understanding is constructed in the larger society of which my informants are a part. This is of course not to say that the tradition that shapes believers' narratives is unimportant, so I would like to turn now to a brief background sketch on Evangelical Christianity and the conversion narrative.

Evangelical Christianity

The term "evangelical" must be understood in historical and polemical contexts. "Evangelical" takes its contemporary meaning from a long history of controversies within Christianity that concern very basic principles of faith. Although the term is used in the New Testament, its polemical significance stems from the Reformation period, when it was used first of all by Luther to contrast his form of religiosity to the more ritual and tradition-based form that characterized the Roman church (Gerstner 1975: 23). The term gained more specificity during the seventeenth and eighteenth centuries in the confrontation between orthodox Protestants and a new set of reformers, the Pietists (Stoeffler 1965; Stromberg 1986). Pietists varied in their particular theological emphases as much as had earlier Protestants, but a general principle of the movement was the stress on the need for an experiential faith as opposed to one based in doctrine. Pietists of all varieties, in other words, emphasized and perhaps intensified the fundamental Protestant message that it is the faith of the individual rather than the saving efficacy of the church that is necessary for a valid Christianity. In some varieties of Pietism, this experiential focus took the form of an insistence that the believer must personally undergo a "born again" experience in which his or her commitment to Christ was affirmed (Pinson 1934).

The tenet that religion must be a matter between the individual and God is closely associated with another principle in most varieties of Christianity that choose the label "Evangelical." If it is above all the experience of the individual that may create a significant link to the divine, there must be some channel, other than the church, through which God may communicate personally with the believer. In the Evangelical tradition this channel is the Bible.

It is above all in the United States that a broad religious tradition calling itself "Evangelical" developed. The historical conditions for this development – which are described at length in James Hunter's (1983) study of American Evangelicalism – were the increasing influence of modern ideas in realms of ethics, science and Biblical criticism. During the decades around the turn of the twentieth century, strong currents within American Protestantism, in response to such ideas, shaped a more liberal, socially active Christianity less committed to Biblical literalism than had been the case in the nineteenth century. American Fundamentalism and contemporary Evangelicalism grew out of a conservative backlash against this "New Christianity" (Hunter 1983). In contrast to that part of Protestantism that has sought to assimilate modernity, Evangelicalism has tended to continue to affirm the inspired and infallible character of the Scriptures. As expressed by a contemporary Evangelical theologian, "Scripture, as illumined by the Holy Spirit, is the only trustworthy guide in moral and spiritual matters" (Kantzer 1975: 78).

Contemporary American Evangelicalism, then, reflects a dogged attempt to defend certain basic principles of the experiential tradition in Protestantism in the face of the threat of modernity. In practice, this attempt can be summarized in three basic principles. To quote Hunter (1983: 7):

At the doctrinal core, contemporary Evangelicals can be identified by their adherence to (1) the belief that the Bible is the inerrant Word of God, (2) the belief in the divinity of Christ, and (3) the belief in the efficacy of Christ's life, death and physical resurrection for the salvation of the human soul.

In much of the Evangelical tradition, the third principle takes the form of a stress upon the importance of an experience of commitment to Christ through a personal conversion experience. Although such an experience was not a requirement for membership at the church I studied, all church members I spoke with regarded it as an important component of faith. In practice, of course, what is required is not so much a conversion – by its nature a transformation of the soul that occurs outside of the public view – as a conversion narrative.

The question of what counts as a conversion narrative, of how the genre of the conversion narrative is defined, is unfortunately little researched. Apart from the interesting work of Patricia Caldwell (1983) on Puritan conversion narratives, I know of no detailed studies of the conversion narrative as a genre. Even worse, it is not possible to offer such an analysis based on my own data, which were not collected with such a goal in mind. Thus I cannot answer such important questions as: What counts as a conversion narrative (either in a particular group or in Evangelicalism as a whole)? How do believers learn to tell conversion narratives? Are there variations in conversion narratives across time or social groups? Are there themes that characterize conversion stories no matter what the historical context?

These questions must await further research. For the moment, I will note only that in the very large congregation I studied, there was no "witnessing" in front of the entire congregation, a practice that would tend to shape conversion stories around a particular form. There were, on the other hand, opportunities to relate conversion stories in smaller groups such as adult Sunday school classes or with groups of friends. My impression from participating in church activities and interviewing members is that there was little pressure toward standardization of narratives, that a believer's story of conversion was unlikely to be questioned as inadequate by other members.

Although a fuller understanding of the generic features of the conversion narrative would be helpful as background to the present work, its absence will not in any way compromise the study. My concern here is with the ways in which believers integrate a shared religious language into the idiosyncratic details of their own life histories and situations, a topic that can be studied without extensive knowledge of the generic features of the conversion story. The central task of the believer in Evangelical Christianity is, through his or her interpretation of Scripture, to find a meaningful link between the symbol system (the Bible) and his or her experience. The conversion narrative is the creation of this link through language, and it is therefore to the nature of language that I must now turn.

The referential

I want to discuss some general assumptions about language, but the situation is complicated by the fact that I will eventually argue that the conversion narrative both exists and is effective because of certain pervasive ideas about language and persons in our society, *ideas that are shared not only by the believers I will discuss but by many of the readers of this book*.[4]

These pervasive – and in my view, implausible – assumptions about language can be summarized using a term suggested by Michael Silverstein (1979), that being "linguistic ideology." By this term Silverstein means to refer to a set of pervasive and nearly unquestionable assumptions in a culture about how language works. Such assumptions are not, as might first seem the case, only of concern to dreamy intellectuals. Rather, ideas about meaning in language inform much everyday reasoning

As noted earlier, Silverstein points out that English speakers, and probably speakers of Indo-European languages in general, subscribe to a referential[5] view of language.[6] By this he means that speakers of English assume that language works because linguistic symbols – words – convey discrete and specific meanings. English speakers, in other words, foreground referential functions of language at the expense of pragmatic functions. This outlook can be observed, for example, in the conviction that communication happens because words are associated with specifiable referential meanings that can be clearly delineated, as they are in dictionaries.

In spite of the fact that the referential view seems unassailable, the clearest sort of common sense, it is not a very good theory of meaning-creation in language. In the first place, no philosopher or linguist has ever come up with a widely accepted account of how these referential meanings get attached to words. Second, as noted, the referential ideology considerably underplays the role of indexical processes – processes that depend upon the relationship between sign and context – in communication.

Third, the referential ideology sets up a host of philosophical problems by positing language as a medium between the ideas of a core self and an external reality. These problems have to do with the nature of the self, of external reality, and the ability of language to express either one of these. As noted, these questions do not only provide employment for philosophers, in one form or another they engage most members of our society. As I will argue at length below, how we think about persons and their place in the world is closely bound up with the referential ideology of language.

The mysteries generated by the referential ideology of language have considerable practical import, because they affect how people understand themselves, their neighbors, their societies, and their universe. The conversion narrative is one example of a ritual that attempts to address and resolve certain contradictions entailed in the referential ideology so that people can live their lives in a way they find meaningful. To study this ritual, one must remain alert to the existence and importance of the referential ideology while avoiding being drawn into its assumptions. The study of the conversion narrative must take place within the framework of an alternative view of language.

Much of philosophy and social science during this century can be seen as an attempt to construct such an alternative. Analytical philosophy after Wittgenstein's later work, ethnomethodology, and sociolinguistics are entire schools of thought dedicated in part to the task of attacking the referential ideology. However, even much of the work that has attempted to offer alternatives to the referential ideology has continued to reify referential processes under the rubric of meanings. The attack on the referential ideology, for example, may be carried out by pointing to the importance of "indexical meaning."

Although it is probably not possible for any work of social science, including this one, to give up the idea of meaning, it may be possible to give up the idea of meanings as mysterious essences conveyed between language-users by words. Richard Rorty (1989: 10), for example (following Donald Davidson), urges us to do this by abandoning the notion that language is a medium for expression or representation. But when one considers this suggestion, it seems unhelpful. Does Rorty really want to give up the idea that language conveys, say, ideas? Why would one write articles on language if one took such a position seriously?

The question here has to do with the idiom used to discuss meaning processes in language, for the questions one will be led to ask are closely tied to that idiom. For many purposes it may be harmless to talk about language as conveying ideas. However, language is not a mystical system that somehow links noises and gestures to specifiable mental contents, nuggets we call ideas or beliefs or meanings. Language is nothing other than human activity, in Rorty's (1987) phrase, "familiar noises." Humans can communicate because they are able to commit many associations to memory, but also because they are always able to modify those associations in different contexts. Communication happens, in philosopher Donald Davidson's (1986: 442) terms, based on a temporary convergence in "passing theories" held by speaker and interpreter.

Passing theories are not the grand and systematic grammars often assumed to underlie language-use. Rather they are *ad hoc* strategies for making sense of another's (or one's own) behavior. A passing theory is my understanding of what you mean in a particular utterance. That theory is based upon my prior knowledge of the language we speak but it is not the same as that prior knowledge, for you might – in fact you probably will – behave in some way that is not covered by that prior knowledge. As Rorty (1989: 14) writes:

Such a theory is "passing" because it must constantly be corrected to allow for mumbles, stumbles, malapropisms, metaphors, tics, seizures, psychotic symptoms, egregious stupidity, strokes of genius, and the like.

To say that communication is dependent upon a convergence in passing theories between speaker and hearer is to say that there is never an overarching system or code which is brought by language-users into a situation and which can completely account for communication. As Davidson puts it, rather provocatively, "there is no such thing as a language, not if a language is anything like what many philosophers and linguists have supposed" (1986: 446).

I would put it differently: Language is not the system it is presumed to be in the referential ideology. It is important to realize, however, that to say that the referential ideology is not a good explanation of language is not to deny that referential processes exist and are central to human communication. That is, it is of course true that communication depends upon largely consensual associations to familiar noises and gestures. Such a process plays a role in language, but it is not the explanation of language. English speakers are continuously tempted to *reify* one aspect of human communicative behavior – the linkage of common associations to familiar symbols – and to regard it as the *explanation* of human communicative behavior, and it is this that I am arguing against.

From this perspective, then, what appear as referential meanings are simply areas of stability in the constantly fluctuating use of communicative symbols. Once one has gotten beyond the habit of attributing to these areas a real existence, one can then grant their significance as *patterns of use*. That is, referential processes are regularities in use that are of enormous social import. Although I risk sounding hyperbolic by saying it, "the referential" is part of the very foundation of our social order. The social process that defines, from moment to moment, our continuously evolving sense of what it is possible to express defines the limits of our immediate imagination.

By "the referential" I mean to designate communicative behavior that proceeds within the confines of the familiar. The referential is, in any society, the domain of the sayable. Within these boundaries, passing theories converge to such an extent that members of the society are easily convinced that their actions express underlying realities they call "meanings." When symbols are used in a manner that conveys a consensual meaning within a community, I will say those symbols are being used referentially.

The constitutive

Many anthropologists have identified culture with the realm of the referential, defining culture as a system of shared assumptions about and interpretations of the world. The referential could also be equated with what some philosophers have called "the realm of literal meaning." Consider, for example, Richard Rorty (1987: 285) discussing his colleagues Davidson and Quine:

semantical notions like 'meaning' have [for Davidson] a role only within the quite narrow (though shifting) limits of regular, predictable, linguistic behaviour – the limits which mark off (temporarily) the literal use of language. In Quine's image, the realm of meaning is a relatively small 'cleared' area within the jungle of use, one whose boundaries are constantly being both extended and encroached upon.

In this image, the cleared area exists *within* the jungle of use. This reiterates what I have stressed above, namely that communication within the realm of the referential remains nothing other than use, nothing other than human activity. But if a group of people reifies the referential function of communicative behavior, so that meanings seem to have a real existence, the fact that all communicative behavior is ultimately nothing other than use will be obscured. In such a situation, one's interest is focused upon "what is being said" so that the activity of saying often becomes trivial. What is important is "what is said"; "how it is said" is often thought not to matter.

There are, of course, certain sorts of communicative behavior that remain visible as activity even within the referential ideology. Gesture is an example of this. I can say "that was sweet of him" while adopting an ironic expression that will be taken to invert the face-value meaning of what I am saying. Here activity matters; how I make the expression is relevant to the meaning I create. Another example is communication that occurs through symbolic systems other than verbal language. I might choose to convey the message that I am wealthy not by announcing my net worth in public gatherings but rather by purchasing an expensive automobile.

I will designate communicative behaviors that are visible as activities, in which one communicates by doing something, as "constitutive" communicative behaviors, and their properties will be central to the argument of this book.[7] I have chosen the term constitutive because these behaviors always entail, in one way or another, a collapse between communication and situation. Consider, for example, the class of constitutive behaviors that are sometimes called indexical signs, those parts of an utterance that point to some aspect of the spatio-temporal context in which the utterance occurs (Peirce 1932: 143). For example, the "deictics," words such as "this" and "later," are referential indexes in that their specific meanings derive from the contexts in which they occur. For this reason, referential indexes cannot be said to convey abstract associated meanings; their meanings depend upon the contexts in which they are spoken.

To say that some communicative behaviors depend upon the context in which they are spoken is also to say that these behaviors establish contexts, they create situations. For example, many languages have formal and informal second-person pronouns, as English did until a few centuries ago. If I am speaking, say, German, I have a choice; I may refer to you as *Sie* or *Du*. My choice will depend upon our relationship as it manifests itself in a particular context. The formal/informal pronoun choice is thus indexical, in that it points to an aspect of context, the social relationship between speaker and listener. But this fact may also be viewed from the other direction: my choice of formal or informal pronoun not only depends upon, but also constitutes the social relationship between my interlocutor and me. If at some point I shift to the informal, or if I choose over three decades never to do so, I am nevertheless continually constituting our relationship.[8]

Some constitutive behavior occurs within the realm of the referential. That is, there are constitutive behaviors with consensual interpretations. For example, as Austin (1962) pointed out, there is a class of statements – performatives – which are carried out in being said. If I say "I promise" I have promised; situation merges with communication. Other constitutive behavior occurs outside of the realm of the referential, in the uncleared part of Quine's jungle of use. These behaviors may or may not be recognized as communicative, but in any case they have no consensual interpretations; these behaviors, at least initially, make no sense. The argument of this book turns on the relationship between these two classes of constitutive behavior; the model for the first is canonical language, the model for the second is metaphor.

Canonical language

Roy Rappaport (1977: 179) suggests that rituals always consist of two sorts of messages. The first sort of message is what he calls "indexical," information concerning the present state of the participants. The second sort of message is "canonical," information linked to "enduring aspects of nature, society, or cosmos, and ... encoded in apparently invariant aspects of liturgical orders" (ibid.: 182). Broadly speaking, ritual works by effecting exchanges between these two levels, so that the canonical and the immediate are brought into contact (cf. also Geertz 1964).

As was noted above, the conversion narrative is a practice through which believers seek to establish some connection between the language of Evangelical Christianity and their own immediate situations. In other words, the believer who would have a conversion must learn to understand experience and the Word of God in the same terms; some point of tangency must be established where the canonical language and experience merge. In this sense, the admonition to seek a conversion is a call to engage in ritual action of the sort that characterizes religions throughout the world. For, as noted, ritual is always a set of activities intended to effect an exchange between the divine and the mundane levels of existence. Ritual is always a point where God and humanity come into contact;

along this dimension the only difference between the conversion and other forms of ritual is that the conversion is focused upon an individual rather than being an overtly communal action.

One would expect that, as a ritual, the conversion narrative would work much as other rituals do, and indeed this is what I will argue. Central to this argument is the contention that the canonical and the immediate, which are somehow brought into contact in the ritual, are both likely to manifest themselves as constitutive phenomena. Recent approaches to ritual analysis have suggested that to the extent that ritual accomplishes its goals, this success may be most usefully traced to the performative aspects of the ritual (Rappaport 1977, Tambiah 1988). In the words of Edward Schieffelin (1985: 709):

ritual language and ritual modes of communication are not effective mainly because they convey information, reveal important cultural truths, or transform anything on the semantic level. Rather, they are compelling because they establish an order of actions and relationships between the participants through restricting and prescribing the forms of speaking (and I would add, interaction) in which they can engage so that they have no alternative way to act. The situation itself is coercive.

Ritual accomplishes its goals to the extent that it is able to make the canonical constitutive. Ritual works, at least in part, as does a performative utterance: a social state is established in the carrying out of the communication. In this way the canonical, the most certain and unquestionable of meanings, is brought into an immediate and ongoing situation. As Rappaport (1977: 192) comments, it is this that makes ritual perhaps the most fundamental social mechanism for establishing the taken-for-granted, the center of the referential:

It is plausible to suggest . . . that ritual, in the very structure of which authority and acquiescence are implicit, was the primordial means by which men, divested of genetically determined order, established the conventions by which they order themselves.

This "conventionalizing" aspect of ritual, however, is only half of the story. For – and this fact has perhaps been somewhat neglected in the social scientific study of ritual – in addition to bringing the canonical into the moment, ritual also brings the moment into the canonical (Geertz 1964). This brings me to a discussion of the other class of constitutive behavior mentioned above, represented by metaphor.

Metaphor

In some ways, the class of constitutive behavior I take metaphor to represent is directly opposed to canonical language. Whereas the canonical is that with the most established meaning, metaphor is language with no established meaning. I must be clear at the outset about two features of the way I use the term "metaphor" that will set my account off from most other treatments. First, I follow Davidson (1984) and Rorty (1987, 1991) in using the term to refer to a rhetorical figure that has no conventional meaning. I do *not* use the term "metaphor" (as do, say, Lakoff and Johnson [1980]) to refer to long-familiar figures such as "things are looking up."

A metaphor, in the way I will define the term, is a new use of language. It appears, to return once again to Quine's image of the jungle of use, on the borders of the cleared area. As the metaphor is interpreted, the boundaries of the cleared area change. Something becomes articulable that previously was hidden. In a metaphor words are used in an unfamiliar way, but in a way that can be construed as sensible. If the metaphor is successful, those who encounter it get a sense of an original and compelling meaning. Something new has been brought within the confines of the referential, of the sayable and thus conceiveable.

Second, I will often use the term "metaphor" to refer not specifically to a rhetorical figure but rather to a class of communicative behaviors that I take metaphor to represent. That is, I take metaphor to be the paradigm for a whole range of communicative phenomena that may be characterized as "initially opaque to interpretive effort." Such phenomena may occur in areas such as speech dysfluencies, psychological symptoms, religious and artistic symbolism, and so on.

These phenomena are constitutive because they are communications consisting purely in the realm of situation; they are simply things people do. The situation created is the communication; as in all constitutive phenomena one cannot talk about a "meaning" separate from the situation that is created. Of course, any of these phenomena may be interpreted, they may be drawn within the realm of the referential, and it then becomes possible to talk (or perhaps argue) about the "meaning" of these phenomena.

In the ritual of the conversion narrative, these opaque behaviors are reformulated in terms of the canonical language. It is this I referred to above as "bringing the moment into the canonical." Thus it should be noted that the two sorts of communicative behaviors I intend to focus on can both be said to occur on the borders of what I have called the constitutive and the referential. In the conversion narrative, the canonical

– that with the most established of referential meanings – becomes constitutive, while the metaphoric – that with no meaning – comes to be interpretable.

Put differently, in ritual one observes the workings of – as Rappaport and others have noted – two sorts of communication, which I will call the canonical and the metaphoric. The canonical is the referential becoming constitutive and the metaphoric is the constitutive becoming referential. Through the interplay of these two sorts of communicative phenomena, *shifts between the referential and the constitutive* may occur. This book offers examples of such shifts in the ritual of the conversion narrative and attempts to demonstrate that it is through these shifts that self-transformation and increased commitment may occur. More specifically, as the canonical becomes constitutive, aspects of religious symbolism come to be real for believers. And as the metaphoric becomes referential, heretofore mysterious behaviors come to be replaced by religious convictions. The details of how these processes transpire will be examined through a detailed look at the performance of the conversion narrative.

The conversion narrative as performance

Normally the conversion is viewed (both by believers and by students of the conversion) as an historical, observable event that is referred to in the conversion narrative. (See, for example, James 1902.) It is furthermore assumed that the transformational efficacy of the conversion experience occurs in the original event. From the believer's perspective, that event was a miracle, a moment in which God intervened in a demonstrable way in the believer's life. The subsequent change in the believer's life evidences the miraculous nature of the event. In this sense, the conversion conforms to the pattern of the appearance of Jesus Christ in history: it is a moment when history embodies the divine. The very logic of the conversion experience, from the perspective of the believer, necessitates the claim that it is an historical event, the conversion, that transforms the believer.

The social scientist must take a different approach, in part because he or she must bracket the miraculous nature of the event. But even more fundamentally, the social scientist has no direct access to the original conversion event. As I suggested above, even if one assumes no conscious intent by the narrator to deceive, the relationship between the conversion story and the original conversion event is problematic.[9] A conversion experience is a combination of historical events and the person's immediate and subsequent reactions to those events. The analyst cannot assume that the events narrated in the conversion story simply happened in the way the narrator claims, in part because much of the story may reflect emotional reactions which have taken shape since the time of conversion. Any analysis based on the assumption that the conversion narrative may be taken to refer unproblematically to a conversion event is seriously flawed.

A conversion narrative, on the other hand, is an observable event. Unlike the conversion it presumably depicts, the narrative is immediately available as evidence to the researcher. Thus if one wants to study the conversion experience, one is better off looking first to the conversion narrative, and exercising caution about inferences concerning events the narrative presumably describes. In particular, if the conversion has some efficacy in bringing about commitment and self-transformation, the source of that efficacy should be sought first of all in the conversion narrative.

Thus, rather than claiming to study the original conversion event to which believers point, I focus here on the conversion story. One gains a certain amount of precision in adopting such an approach, for no social scientist is likely to ever have a record of a conversion event.[10] Furthermore, one loses very little in adopting an explicit focus on the conversion story, for the conversion story manifests the same emotional themes and transformations that are said to have characterized the original conversion event. In order to tell the stories of their conversions, believers must talk about aspects of their experience that have profound meaning for them. To talk about things that are profoundly meaningful is, by the nature of talk, to portray and betray much of one's feelings about those things, to communicate on various levels the meanings those things have (Goffman 1981).

Even if a person has changed, traces of what he was are likely to manifest themselves in his talk. This is because change is constituted above all in talk, in different habits of formulating, understanding, and speaking. Thus one may expect an interview about a life transition to replay to some extent the drama that it tells about, even if that drama occurred decades earlier. Indeed, it is fair to say that a change in the believer's life is sustained only to the extent that it is continually constituted. Thus, the signs of the transformation taking place should be present in the telling of the story.

In the individualistic form of the conversion ritual, what is established and acted out in the narrative is a particular form of identity (a term I will define in the next chapter). This leads to the conclusion that while the conversion is often effective in transforming the believer's life – as believers claim – this effect is not due to a one-time transformation of the self. In part here the point is that a gradual transformation of identity may take place as a believer learns over time to construe herself and her life in terms of the canonical language. But it is also true – and this is the process I want to investigate in this book – that a particular identity may be acted out in the very performance of the conversion narrative. In other words, I want to suggest that the conversion works in much the same way any ritual works: a ritual creates a particular social reality (Rappaport 1977); in the case of the conversion this social reality is a particular identity.

Constitutive behavior and the subject

In order to begin to explicate the relationship between the conversion narrative and the transformation of the self, I must make some observations on the role of the subject in constitutive behavior.

I have noted that some constitutive behaviors take place within the realm of the referential – that they have widely shared associations – while other constitutive behaviors take place outside that realm, and thus seem initially senseless. It is interesting to note that even some constitutive behaviors with consensual associations are, within the referential ideology of language, not thought to define meaning with certainty. By this I mean that these behaviors are thought to convey meanings that are more subtle and ambiguous than those conveyed by "plain statements." Thus, in the examples of the gesture and the purchase of the automobile, I might deny my ironic gesture on questioning or insist that I purchased the automobile not because I wanted to display my wealth but because its high quality in fact made it a thrifty investment. To use a term suggested by Labov and Fanshel (1977: 46), certain sorts of constitutive communications are "deniable communications." The producer of the behaviors may deny that these actions are communications at all.

Such communications are deniable because of the way the subject is thought to be involved in communication in the referential ideology. Although I will have a great deal more to say on this below, the referential ideology posits a "core self" that expresses its beliefs, feelings, observations, needs, etc. through language. Language has meaning because it corresponds to these states of the core self (and to states of the outside world, although that is less relevant here). Action is communicative if it is selected by the core self. If certain actions may not have been chosen in this way, they may not have been communications.

It should be clear from these observations that the referential ideology of language entails a particular view of the speaking subject. It will be necessary to outline and criticize that view in order to prepare the way for discussing the conversion narrative.

2   Character and intention

The referential ideology of language entails a particular view of the subject in which meaning is tied to the subject's intentions. Like the referential ideology itself, this view of the subject is likely to be taken for granted in our society, to be regarded as common sense. I will use the term common sense to mean that which is obvious, articulable, and taken for granted in a society. Common sense is thus a part of what I have called the referential, that part that may be formulated in widely accepted propositions. In this chapter I will discuss an important part of our society's common-sense view of the subject and language, a number of interlocking assumptions that I will call the "character and intention" system.

Common sense and conversion

The fit between common sense and actual experience is never a perfect one. People's experience often falls outside of what their language and culture might lead them to suspect. This is not only because experience is quite varied. More fundamentally, the fact that common sense makes some things obvious means that common sense makes other things mysterious. If it is obvious that human beings are self-sufficient individuals, then the collective aspects of human life will seem mysterious; if it is obvious that science is the true path to knowledge, then artistic or intuitive modes of knowledge will seem mysterious, and so on. In making sense of some things, a system of thought will obscure other things.

Conversion narratives occur in our society because of what is common sense in our society and what is consequently mysterious. In particular, the conversion narrative can be seen as a ritual generated around certain contradictions in our conceptions of character and intention. These contradictions manifest themselves in a believer's life as personal suffering, and the believer's attempt to address this suffering draws her into that which cannot be understood in terms of common sense. This attempt is to be understood, from the perspective adopted here, as a process of using language to extend the boundaries of common sense, to bring something that cannot be understood within the confines of the familiar. If the attempt is successful, something that has been mysterious becomes articulable, and a profound sense of meaning is generated.

Since the conversion narrative can be seen as a ritual response to contradictions in our common sense, it is therefore important to say something about what those contradictions are. Unfortunately, the content of our own common sense is not a topic on which there can be said to be a scholarly consensus.[1] In describing the system of character and intention, I must rely not upon a well-established literature but rather upon the reader's own familiarity with that system. That is, readers who are sufficiently familiar with Western culture and with the English language to be reading this book should be able to quite capably evaluate my description on the basis of their own intuitions and experience.

I presume that my reason for focusing on the notion of "character" here is clear enough; the conversion is, as noted, explicitly defined by believers as a self-transformation, a change in what one *is*. My interest in intention is perhaps not as easily understood. What does intention have to do with the conversion?

Instead of intention I could probably just as easily talk about "free will" or "volition" or "agency." The point would remain the same: if someone is to transform her character, she must change what she *wants* to do. To be something different is, in the end, to do something differently. This creates a mystery in Western societies, where desires are understood as elemental: how can one want to change what one wants? What one desires is, in our understanding, the bottom line. As Roy D'Andrade (1990: 105) phrases this point, "the very core of the self is its *intentions*, from which it cannot be separated." By what mechanism, then, does one dip below a desire and undermine it so that it can be replaced by a more desirable desire?

The problem of self-transformation entails the problem of will. In a society that regards intention as the ultimate mover in human affairs, a society whose entire moral system is based upon the proposition that people may choose their actions, the transformation of intention is unfathomable. There must be a level of human activity more basic than the will, and yet there cannot be. In this situation, where one has reached the limits of the sayable, one may expect to find the constitutive, as people attempt to go beyond that which can be spoken. The conversion narrative is a ritual mechanism that occurs along this fault line in Western common sense.

There is, of course, an extensive literature on intention in philosophy and other disciplines. I will, for the most part, stay away from this literature. My goal is not to establish what might be ultimately true of human intention – although eventually I hope to offer a new way of talking about intention – but rather at this point merely to review some of our society's common-sense notions of what intention is.

Character and intention

Perhaps the first characterization of intentional action that may occur to the English speaker is that intentional acts are divided from unintentional behaviors by the fact that the former are reflective while the latter are not. That is, if I do something intentionally, I consciously reflect and elect to do that thing. If my behavior proceeds without such reflection, it is not, or is not fully, intentional.

Because intentional acts are reflective they are thought to fairly represent whatever it is in the person that reflects; we are *responsible* for that which we do intentionally. Elizabeth Anscombe (1963: 24) captures this overlap between reflection and responsibility in her formulation that for English speakers intentional actions are those to which the question "why did you do that?" may be applied. One may, she points out, behave in ways to which the question "why" does not apply. For example, I may sneeze. Or I may, in reaching for the bread, upset my water glass. In these cases the question "why" does not apply, so we say that I did not intend to sneeze or spill my water.[2]

In saying that one may ask "why" of an intentional action, Anscombe may be read as saying that intentional action is that which may be connected to a *project* in some construable way.[3] It could turn out, for example, that my spilling the water was in fact a signal to someone else at the table. Perhaps my wife and I have cooked up a sort of code to which we resort in desperate social circumstances, and spilling a glass of water signifies "we've got to get out of here." In this case it would emerge that what had initially seemed an unintentional behavior turns out to have been intentional. And of course, I may have spilled my water "just for the hell of it" (Anscombe 1963: 25). This is also a socially construable project; sometimes people do things for no reason at all, and this is accepted as a reason for acting.

If a behavior can be linked to a project, it is thought to represent whatever it is in the human organism that constructs projects. In other words, according to our common sense, behavior may be either intentional or unintentional, but only the former sort of behavior reflects the moral qualities of the person who produces it. If I normally walk with confidence and grace but happen to trip at a party and spill my drink on a bystander, he will likely be annoyed and I will be sorry, but he will not make a moral judgment of me. That is, I may be judged clumsy or inept, but I will not be judged on any moral dimension (as evil, aggressive, uncompromising, etc.). Because my behavior is unintentional, it is not thought to reflect upon my moral character.

Perhaps one might argue that in some instances I would be held morally accountable for an unintentional behavior. It might turn out, for example, that the drink I spilled was my tenth, in which case the victim might make a moral judgment of me. This observation, however, merely confirms my point. To the extent that my behavior and its immediate context contain an element that may be construed as proceeding from reflection (choosing each successive drink), I am morally accountable.

I am arguing, in sum, that when we say an act is intentional, we usually mean that it proceeds out of reflection and that the person who produces the act can be held accountable for it. Under certain circumstances, however, the connection between intention, reflection, and responsibility seems not to hold. Specifically, there are reflective behaviors for which one may not be held responsible, and which therefore may be construed as unintentional. Likewise, there are unreflective behaviors for which one may accept responsibility and which therefore may be construed as intentional.

An example of the former situation is the behavior of those who can reflect, but perhaps cannot reflect competently. English speakers are uncertain whether to attribute moral responsibility to persons who may have a compromised capacity for reflection, as is evidenced by the existence of the insanity defense. Some such provision is a long-standing component of the Western legal tradition; consider the following passage from the Justinian code of sixth-century Rome: "There are those who are not to be held accountable, such as a madman and a child, who are not capable of wrongful intention" (Carrither 1985: 23; cited in Simon and Aaronson 1988: 10). In the United States, the attempted assassination of Ronald Reagan by John Hinckley provoked a new round of debate on this issue, leading some states to allow for a "guilty but mentally ill" verdict (Simon and Aaronson 1988: 23). But the core principle of the defense, although challenged, has remained intact. That is, as formulated in a statement issued by the American Psychiatric Association:

The insanity defense rests upon one of the fundamental premises of the criminal law, that punishment for wrongful deeds should be predicated upon moral culpability. However, within the framework of English and American law, defendants who lack the ability (the capacity) to rationally control their behavior do not possess free will. They cannot be said to have "chosen to do wrong." Therefore, they should not be punished or handled similarly to all other criminal defendants. (Simon and Aaronson 1988: 20)

One may act after reflecting, but the reflecting itself may be irrational. In such a case it is arguable whether the act is intentional or whether the actor is responsible for the act. Another sort of ambiguously intentional behavior is that which one does not produce reflectively, but for which the person may accept responsibility. Following philosopher of science Michael Polanyi (1962), such action can be termed "tacit" behavior.[4] As Polanyi [ibid.: 62) points out, such behavior is not a minor part of human activity:

> The unspecifiability of the process by which we . . . feel our way forward accounts for the possession by humanity of an immense mental domain, not only of knowledge but of manners, of laws and of the many different arts which man knows how to use, comply with, enjoy or live by, without specifiably knowing their contents.

For example, in standing near another person and speaking to him, I negotiate a precise distance that can be shown to be socially determined. Although I acknowledge responsibility for this behavior, for the most part it proceeds outside of my consciousness. Again, English speakers might reasonably argue about whether this behavior is intentional or unintentional.

These cases, in which intention does not seem to be tied to reflection, do not contradict my contention that for the most part what English speakers mean by intentional action is behavior which is reflective and hence behavior for which the actor bears responsibility. The point is that these cases *arguably* concern intentional action, and as such divert one from the heart of what is meant by intentional action. A short digression into recent work in cognitive science will clarify my point here.

As was pointed out above, there is always some divergence between the referential, the world as it is supposed to be, and actual experience. One of the great contributions of recent research in cognitive science has been to establish that many words and categories are defined relative to cognitive models that may in fact fit experience rather poorly. That is, words may often take their meaning not from the complexities of the social and natural worlds but rather from simplified *models* of those worlds that are learned along with language. I want to suggest that intention is a word defined with reference to a simplified cognitive model.

Categories that are defined relative to simplified cognitive models will apply better to some parts of the actually-encountered world than others, because some parts of the actually-encountered world are indeed quite like the simplified models, and others are not. As it has been formulated by Rosch (1975; Rosch and Mervis 1975) and her colleagues, many, perhaps all, categories show what George Lakoff (1987) calls "prototype effects." In simple terms, most or all categories are structured not with clear boundaries, but with fuzzy ones. While there are some entities that clearly fit into the category (prototypes) and others that clearly do not, there are also entities whose membership in the category is ambiguous.

This means that categories do not actually function, as English speakers often unreflectively assume, as sets that clearly separate the world into "members" and "non-members." Rather, categories are defined by proto-typical examples, and membership in the category is a matter of how closely an entity resembles that prototype. Thus, to cite an often used example, a robin is a "better" member of the category "bird" than is a penguin.

Another example – by now so widely discussed that it will be redundant for many readers – is the English word "bachelor," first analyzed by Fillmore (1982). Most English speakers will define bachelor roughly as the dictionary does, as an unmarried adult male. Most of these same people will also agree that some unmarried adult males – the Pope, for instance – are very poor examples of a bachelor. The problem is not that the original definition was wrong, for in fact no definition specifying the precise objective characteristics of the bachelor is available. The problem, as Fillmore points out, is rather that the term "bachelor" makes sense relative to a simplified cognitive model of the social world in which all men, upon reaching a certain age, can be expected to marry. Parts of the social world are like that – and in these parts people may speak of bachelors – but other parts are not. As Lakoff (1987: 70) writes in discussing this example:

The idealized model says nothing about the existence of priests, "long term unmarried coupling," homosexuality, Moslems who are permitted four wives and only have three, etc. The term bachelor works well when one is close to the cognitive model, and poorly when one is working with a segment of the social world which diverges from it.

The category "intention" also has a prototypical sense. The "best" examples of intentional action involve reflection; if I soberly reflect upon my alternatives and choose one of them, then surely I have acted intentionally. My act then represents me, I am responsible for my act. However, just as we may be easily made aware that there are situations in the social world to which the concept "bachelor" applies poorly, so we may understand that the model of human action entailed in our common-sense understanding of character and intention is not always adequate. Specifically, there are realms of behavior that are ambiguously intentio-nal, such as tacit behavior and the behavior of the insane. It is nevertheless true that the heart of the matter about intention is that it is reflective action that represents something essential about the actor.

This conclusion suggests certain things about the underlying model of the acting person that shapes the category of intention. It is assumed, in our society, that a properly functioning human being possesses (indeed, is defined by) an ability to deliberately direct his or her behavior. And our moral judgments of a person are presumed to reflect their exercise of this ability. Although behavior may be generated by forces other than this ability – by the body itself, by passions, by a diseased mind, and so on – to the extent that this occurs, no moral judgment is appropriate.

Over time, the exercise of a person's ability to direct her behavior shapes her character. This character represents the constancy and coherence of her agency; it "fits together" and forms the essence of what she is. This largely enduring and coherent character is the source of intentions; and intentions, over time, are the evidence from which character is inferred.

The conversion narrative tells of how the narrator reshaped his character. Any attempt to transform one's character (and thus at base to transform one's very intentions) lands a member of our society in a contradictory situation in which the assumptions and categories of our common sense lead to an impasse. For one's character is what one *is*. If one's choices reflect one's character, how can one begin to make choices that represent another character?[5] This is where constitutive processes enter in. The status quo, the taken for granted and established, must be transcended. Language must be extended beyond the realm of the referential. Of course, in the conversion narrative – as is common in ritual discourse – the constitutive processes at work are rendered *opaque* by a set of ideas that trace the efficacy of those processes to a mysterious and ultimately unknowable agency, that of the divinity. The analysis in this book will trace this efficacy differently; it will be an attempt to explain the role of shifts between constitutive and referential processes in this transformation.

An alternative understanding of character and intention

In order to offer an alternative account of the conversion narrative to that of common sense, I must extend my incipient account of language-use to embrace a new view of intention and character. Fortunately, anthropological work extending over several decades – particularly work done on concepts of person, self, and individual, in other societies – has begun to make it possible for the social scientist to view the assumptions of the character and intention system with a somewhat critical eye.[6] The by-now extensive literature on how people in many parts of the world understand the person in society enables the Western social scientist to imagine alternative approaches to the one within which he or she has been raised.

Once again, the construction of an alternative necessitates close attention to the role of language, for the character and intention system is closely linked to common-sense assumptions about meaning in language. It is central to the common-sense view that a stretch of language allows one to express an intention which is, generally speaking, the meaning of that language. I want to challenge this view by suggesting that the language used by speakers very often conveys meanings they create but do not in a strict sense intend. This claim will require further explanation.

Imagine that in a tape-recorded conversation I hear a person say, "I really admire Frank." Imagine further that upon closer listening, it becomes clear that in producing this utterance the person initially erred in pronouncing "admire," beginning with an "ab" sound and then quickly correcting his mistake. This is of course what Freud (1952: 38ff.) called a slip of the tongue or a parapraxis. If there is corroborating evidence from other sources, it might be argued that the person began to say "abhor," and that this reflects an attitude about Frank that the speaker holds but is unwilling to acknowledge.

I have (following Labov and Fanshel [1977]) suggested the term "deniable communication" to refer to those aspects of an utterance, such as parapraxes, that are conventionally regarded as unintentional. The term is useful because it draws attention to the fact that although some aspect of a communication may not have been consciously intended, it was nevertheless produced by the speaker. Rather than conveying "the speaker did not have the purpose of producing this communication," the term conveys "the speaker denies having the purpose of producing this communication." Much of the material in this book suggests that observers would do well to emulate the carefulness of the second formation. For to say that speakers may communicate certain messages without having any responsibility for doing so is to fall into a language that reinforces undemonstrated common-sense notions about mental and somatic processes.

In the common-sense view, it is assumed that deniable communications are mere noise, errors in speaking that for the most part convey no meaning. Closely connected to this assumption is another, namely that speakers have unambiguous aims that they express through language. That is, the assumption that deniable communications are meaningless directly reflects our underlying conception of a person as an entity with unambiguous aims that he expresses through speech.

Both of these assumptions are misleading. The conviction that speakers have discernible and fully coherent aims seems based in nothing other than common-sense conceptions about mind and character. It seems more plausible to say that language generally allows us to formulate multiple purposes in a single utterance, with what we regard as our "true" purpose depending in part on how our speech is interpreted by ourselves and others in interaction. To adopt this view, however, jeopardizes one's sense of an individual as a coherent and utterly autonomous subject. The assumption that speech directly reflects unambiguous aims, in short, is a corollary to the commitment to a conception of the individual subject as autonomous and coherent.

In contrast to this view, I suggest that subjects be conceptualized as having multiple and sometimes contradictory aims, and that utterances be assumed to accurately reflect this somewhat messy subjectivity. Now the claim that there is a direct connection between intention and meaning takes on a different cast: an utterance does indeed reflect the purposes of a speaker, but these purposes may be unacknowledged ones.

The complex language of "purposes," "aims," and "intentions" here is necessitated by the fact that our language makes certain assumptions bout volition very difficult to avoid. If one wants to convey the idea that a subject is responsible for a behavior, one may select from a fairly rich supply of terms – intention, purpose, aim, goal, plan – all of which imply that the subject is consciously aware of this responsibility. The only way around this implication is to resort to the terminology of, say, unconscious goals. Unfortunately, this terminology implies the acceptance of aspects of psychoanalytic theory that are, I believe, best avoided.[7]

Thus the common sense embedded in our linguistic system, in particular in certain deeply entrenched convictions about the nature of human actors, makes it difficult to describe a speaker's unacknowledged purposes. In this situation I am forced to improvise, to design a terminology appropriate to the task. I will in the first place use the term "intention" to refer to the subject's acknowledged purposes and aims. The two terms "purpose" and "aim" will be used – and this is to some extent counter to common usage – to refer to goals that may or may not be acknowledged. Thus in the example above, the speaker's intention was to express his admiration for Frank, but his purpose may have been less straightforward: in speaking, he may have communicated his unacknowledged dislike for Frank as well as his admiration.

I say that the speaker "may" dislike Frank because his slip is in fact limited evidence for this conclusion, by itself hardly outweighing the speaker's protestations that he holds Frank in the highest regard. This brings me to an important point. The nature of the evidence called upon to demonstrate an unacknowledged purpose is, according to the common-sense understanding of meaning in our society, not particularly relevant to establishing meaning. In the common sense view, the meaning of an utterance is what a speaker intends; if an interlocutor is unsure of a speaker's meaning, she asks the speaker to clarify his meaning by asking him what he intended to say. The assertion that a speaker has created a meaning he does not intend can never, within the framework of the referential ideology of language, be anything other than a hypothesis.

The result of this is that the hypothesis that an utterance expresses an unacknowledged aim can be supported only by a sort of evidence that may be regarded as no evidence at all. One who wishes to demonstrate the existence of meanings beyond intention is consigned to a shadowy realm of processes speakers have been taught to regard as irrelevant, the detritus of speech: changes in tone, pauses, slips of the tongue, patterns of lexical choice, and so on. Speakers generally consign such communications, to use a term from the work of Erving Goffman (1986), to the "disattend track." Thus common-sense ideas of how language is interpreted factor out from the start those sorts of evidence that indicate the ambiguity of a speaker's intentions.

In the character and intention system of our common sense, subjects are defined as entities with coherent intentions. That is, subjects act on the basis of reflection upon their ends; these ends themselves constitute a coherent system that defines the character of the subject. I want to argue that this view of the subject is inaccurate in two ways. First, although subjects indeed have ends, they are not always aware of those ends. Furthermore, the ends of the subject are not coherent, that is, the subject is likely to hold contradictory ends.

This does not mean, however, that I want to abandon any notion that the subject is coherent. I will use the term "identity" because I want to affirm that there is something about the subject that is generally coherent across time and social space. It does not follow from this, however, that identity should be conceived as an essence that exists outside of time and social space. That is, I do not intend identity to be synonymous with character in the common-sense system.

A good model for how identity would best be conceived is style. Style, as in style of movement or style of writing, is something we think of as having coherence over time, yet we do not fall into the assumption that style exists separately from the movements or writing in which it is observed. Style is the coherence of ongoing action, which cannot be abstracted from time. As philosopher of religion Stephen Crites (1971: 292) put it:

An action is altogether temporal. Yet it has a unity of form through time, a form revealed only in the action as a whole. That temporal form is what we mean by style. My gait has a particular style – an ungainly one, as it happens, of a sort developed in walking through cornfields. But you could not detect it in a still photograph, because the style is in the movement.

We think of style as being manifest in activity without being tempted to imagine that it exists separate from activity. Style is a way of doing, and that is precisely how we should think of identity. In fact this analogy is more than an analogy. There is a direct link between style and identity. What we are really talking about when we speak of identity is precisely a style of self-presentation: style of motion, style of interacting, style of talking.[8]

Identity, then, is a congeries of styles, ways of doing things. Although certainly many aspects of identity are available for articulation, they become so only indirectly. That is, we observe ourselves and draw conclusions about who we are rather than thinking continuously, "this is who I am so I shall proceed in this manner." Another way of putting this is to say that much of one's identity is not produced intentionally. The skill of having an identity, like many other skills, is a largely tacit and inarticulate one.

Identity and purpose in the conversion narrative

The argument I am making here about identity and purposes constitutes an attempt to avoid using these concepts in a way that simply reflects the common sense embedded in the verbal categories of English. It is only by doing this, I hold, that the social meaning of the conversion narrative can be understood.

Practices such as the conversion narrative arise as ritual means to reconcile contradictions in common-sense views held by an individual concerning human beings, intentions, morality, and so on. Such contradictions are likely to manifest themselves in our society in experiences of emotional conflict or "mental illness." Thus conversion narratives very often refer to emotional distress, mental illness, or other intense personal conflict as the conditions that preceded and made way for the conversion.

I have been trying to develop a vocabulary for talking about these contradictions that, as much as possible, avoids depending upon common-sense understandings of character and intention. In this connection, perhaps the first thing to note about "mental illness" is that it is recalcitrant to a description in the language of intention. A wide range of symptoms diagnostic of emotional or mental illness have the quality of being ego-alien: the sufferer produces the symptom but has no sense of having intended to do so. From the alternative perspective I am outlining here, this situation occurs because of a contradiction between an actor's self-conception and his identity.

I use the term "self" to refer not to an entity but to an ability, the ability of the human organism to be reflexively aware. While I presume that many animals are aware of aspects of their situations, I presume that only humans are aware of being aware. Whether the basis of this ability is physiological or linguistic (I assume it to be both), its effect is to create a level of experience I will call the self: to say of an organism that it is aware that it is aware that it is hungry is to imagine it capable of understanding "I am hungry."

Because of this ability, human beings are capable of reflecting themselves to themselves; they may create self-conceptions. "I am a college professor. I am better at tennis than I am at polo." Self-conception is presumably in some cases an accurate depiction of identity, in other cases not; people are sometimes misled about themselves. In cases where an unacknowledged aim, a part of identity, directly contradicts the acknowledged intentions of the actor and therefore contradicts the actor's self-conception, that aim will be experienced as ego-alien.

From this perspective, what are sometimes called psychological symptoms should not be traced to the effects of erupting unconscious forces. Rather, they should be understood as the communication, through metaphoric constitutive processes, of aims that are in contradiction with the actor's acknowledged intentions and self-conception. The fact that some aims may be denied by their authors stems from the fact that the organization of behavior, linguistic and otherwise, is a tacit skill. Thus the production of a symptom is not fundamentally different from the exercise of any inarticulate skill: a behavior is produced, and the author of the behavior is for the most part unable to say how or why it was done.

Thus, the sort of bodily disturbance that was once called a "neurotic" symptom – a hysterical paralysis, an obsession, an attack of anxiety – may be reconceived as a constitutive behavior communicating an unacknowledged aim. The symptom, in other words, communicates an aim not by encoding it in the "what is said" of speech but in "how" the subject presents herself as a person (in speech and other communicative activities). The reason these communicative behaviors are often labeled as symptoms is that these behaviors are unconstruable as conveying a socially appropriate intention; they cannot be construed as a part of the referential. The producer of such actions experiences them as ego-alien, since they point to aims she is unwilling to acknowledge.

That unacknowledged aims are communicated through bodily processes follows from the fact that they are excluded from the "what is said", the referential component, of linguistic behavior. In order to stress that I want to attend to the physical part of the subject as well as to the mind that we take speech to imply, I will often refer to unacknowledged purposes as "embodied."[9] In fact, every human act is as embodied as every other, but this terminology will have the advantage of reminding my readers of the common-sense framework that they share with the author and, most importantly, with the subjects who narrate their conversions in this book.

To return now to the question of self-transformation: How, from this perspective, could it happen that a subject could modify or eliminate a symptom? Simply put, I will argue that the self-transformation associated with the conversion occurs as a result of changing embodied aims into articulable intentions, or more accurately, in moving such aims toward the articulable end of the continuum. This movement has the effect of producing a sense of transformation because it draws a new part of the subject's experience into the realm of self. When an embodied aim becomes articulable, it enters the domain of paraphrasability.[10] Embodied aims, through being expressed in a conventionalized language, come to be recognized both by the subject and by interactants as communicative behaviors rather than disturbances in communication.

This leads directly to a paradox that is at the heart of this inquiry. In order to change a behavior that formulates an unacknowledged purpose, the subject must somehow reach into the tacit organization of his or her own behavior, an area that is by definition beyond articulation and thus beyond conscious manipulation. It is, in the end, only through constitutive processes that this can be accomplished. More specifically, such a feat is possible because of shifts between constitutive and referential realms; in the terms suggested above, bringing the constitutive into the cleared area of meaning entails the possibility of changing the boundaries of that cleared area. The possibility of a shift from the constitutive to the referential means that a disruptive communicative behavior may be formulated instead as a statement, in the case of the conversion narrative, usually a statement about faith.

The shift between the constitutive and the referential is facilitated by a canonical language, in this case the language of Evangelical Christianity. In searching for ways to link their personal experience to the formulas of the religion, Evangelical Christians may reformulate the metaphoric in terms of the canonical. Very often, in the narratives, this takes one of two forms. In the first, the believer fulfills a purpose in her relationship with God that is forbidden in other social contexts. In the second, an unacknowledged aim is attributed to God; God does what the believer cannot do. Both of these forms share the same underlying principle: something that is forbidden and unsayable, that must therefore be expressed metaphorically, can be said in terms of the canonical language.

To communicate the otherwise unsayable in the canonical language has two effects. First, unacknowledged purposes are drawn within the referential, the domain of articulation. The sense of revelation or insight that is so often associated with the conversion is simply another version of what happens to any language user who "gets" a metaphor: a previously opaque communication becomes articulable. In the conversion narrative, that opaque communication may involve an undesired behavior, so that its reformulation as religious behavior may entail self-transformation.

Second, as an unacknowledged aim comes to be formulated in terms of the canonical language, the canonical comes to function metaphorically in the special sense I have defined here. The result of this is that a previously referential term may come to have a special significance for the believer, probably manifesting itself on an inarticulate level as a *feeling*. This profound feeling of significance is likely to strengthen the believer's commitment to the canonical language.

A conversion narrative, then, is a ritual that integrates unacknowledged purposes into a socially construable project – namely, being an Evangelical Christian – and thus makes those purposes understandable. Roughly, the point here is akin to that of numerous studies that have pointed out how bizarre behavior of various stripes may become a valued sign of religious grace in the proper context. Prophets and mystics are very often transformed outcasts who have been troubled by hallucinations, recurrent illnesses, masochistic behavior, etc. (Spiro 1965, Wallace 1970).

However, the difficulty and profundity of the transformation from symptom to saintliness has usually been underestimated. It is not simply a matter of getting a few followers to accept one's self-inflicted wounds as stigmata. Rather, the believer who wants to be transformed in this way must somehow divert his or her emotional energy from previous concerns into religious ones; that is, such transformations are effective to the extent that they are genuine (Obeyesekere 1981). Something that has been beyond the domain of the communicable enters into that domain; something that has divided a sufferer from his fellows comes to unite a believer with a community. Thus I hope to show, in looking at several conversion narratives, not only that the believer places certain unacknowledged aims in a religious context, but that in so doing, he or she may really undergo a personal transformation of social and personal significance.

3 Boundaries

Many social scientists share with Evangelical Christians the assumption that what I have called a person's character is the outward manifestation of an inner "true self" that is largely constant across the course of a life. This true self may be modified in extraordinary circumstances, and from that time the self persists in its new, altered state. A religious conversion is often understood as an event which alters the self and thereby transforms character.

As an alternative to this view, I have suggested that the coherence and continuity of a person be conceived as identity, which is not like an inner essence but rather like style, a general consistency in action over time. The conversion, then, is not a one-time transformation of self or character but rather a process that somehow enables a person to act differently. In this chapter I hope to support this claim by showing in a particular case that conflicts that gave rise to the original conversion event persist in the present, in the narration of the conversion story. Although this fact could of course be taken to show that the conversion is in fact not effective as any sort of self-transformation, much evidence contradicts such an interpretation. In particular, both from the perspective of believers and of outside observers, people often do change their behavior after conversions. Thus I suggest an equally plausible interpretation, one that has the advantage of explaining why so many believers testify to the efficacy of conversions: psychological change may occur in certain experiences, but such change is not the one-time alteration of an essence such as character or true self. Rather, change must be constantly re-created. Conflicts do not disappear subsequent to the conversion; instead they come to be approached in a manner that makes their ongoing resolution possible.

The conversion story itself is the most telling evidence for this claim. Upon close examination, there are considerable signs in the story itself of the subject's expressing and then coming to terms with conflicts between contradictory aims. To demonstrate this, however, demands a set of methods that are different from those conventionally used to study conversions. In particular, this task demands methods that will allow the

31

analyst to focus in detail on the conversion narrative and on what is happening as the believer tells her story.

Methods of analysis

Such a focus is compatible with the theoretical stance outlined in the previous chapters, in that by looking at the language of the conversion story one resists the temptation to posit essences such as "character" and "the conversion event" that dwell in some unobservable realm. What any social scientist encounters in doing research is a situation: a ritual, a subject filling out a questionnaire, an interview. Rather than abstracting entities from that situation – entities such as personality, culture, or social structure – one may turn to the situation itself.

Any social situation is at once a product of the social and cultural resources that participants bring into the situation and of the unique exigencies of that particular moment of history. In order to understand the practices through which persons communicate and create a social life, one must begin with the situations in which social actors are observed. It is not true, as functionalist social science often assumed, that the situation can be ignored. It is also not true, as certain radical versions of symbolic interactionist thought have held, that there are no social regularities beyond social situations themselves. Rather, in doing analysis in social science, one must attend both to what I have called the referential and the constitutive. Patterns and regularities – in society, in culture, in identity – are the basis of communication. But there is no short-cut to isolating such regularities; they can be sought only by wading into the complexity of particular social situations.[1]

This conviction underlies the choice of methods used for analyzing data in this book. In the first place, although my research on the conversion entailed the use of a number of methods of gathering information, including the use of survey questionnaires, I have chosen to use only interview material in this book. All interviews were conducted by the author, and although I often resorted to similar questions in different interviews, I made no attempt to administer a particular set of questions. Rather, my goal was to give my interlocutor every opportunity to tell me the story of how he or she had come to faith. In some cases, this story did not revolve around a particular moment of transformation, but what the subject told me is not any less a conversion narrative for that reason. I thus use the term "conversion narrative" to refer to the sum total of what my subjects said to me in the course of an open-ended interview explicitly entered upon to allow the subject to tell the story of his or her conversion.

I have had some training in clinical interviewing techniques, and the way I conducted the interviews undoubtedly reflected that experience.[2] In particular I sought to determine, as I spoke with subjects, what topics seemed most emotionally salient for them, and I encouraged them to discuss those topics. I tried to attend closely to what my interlocutors were trying to tell me, and often made an attempt to rephrase their statements, both to make sure I had understood them and to reassure them that I was indeed listening. I sought to attend not only to their reactions to the ongoing situation, but to my own, to keep track of how I was responding to this person and what that might mean for the interview.

As recent studies of interviewing have forcefully pointed out, the meaning of the interview for the respondent is likely to be quite different from its meaning for the researcher. It is often the case that interviewer and respondent are operating under different sets of assumptions about just what social situation they are creating (Briggs 1986). Part of the difficulty in conducting and interpreting interviews is to set aside one's prejudices about what is going on in order to make some room for the respondent's definition of the situation. As a first step, in this research it is necessary to keep in mind that what I construe as an interview is likely to be for the respondent an opportunity to witness about the validity of his or her faith.

A second principle of method guiding this work is my choice to present only a small number of conversion narratives and to examine them in considerable depth. Although I endorse the goal of offering generalizations about particular populations and about human social life in general, the path to such generalizations is more difficult to travel than many social scientists have assumed. Many of those currently studying religious conversion, for example, remain committed to methods in which large numbers of respondents are surveyed through such devices as questionnaires. The material thus collected is often presented with little or no attention to the situation in which it was collected, and with little or no acknowledgement of the fact that respondents may choose similar answers to questions while meaning quite different things by those answers. The number of such studies runs into the hundreds, perhaps thousands. Having myself read a certain proportion of this literature, I cannot avoid the conclusion that were a candid outsider to offer an appraisal of the decisive findings or the important insights that have been gained through such work, that appraisal would not be very enthusiastic. While I urge those committed to this sort of research to continue their efforts – let no stone remain unturned in the pursuit of knowledge! – surely the time has come to seriously pursue some alternative approaches. Alongside the countless studies that survey a large number of converts in an attempt to determine their "objective" similarities, it surely cannot hurt to have a few studies that try to attend, in detail, to what converts say and how they say it. Although it would be best to do this for a large number of cases, the goal of volume is in direct contradiction to that of detailed attention, given the fact that there are limits to a reader's patience. Thus I have chosen to give myself the space I need to explain what I think is important about a few narratives, and I hope that if this sort of analysis proves persuasive, then further work can tackle the problem of how generalizable these results might be.

A third principle of method arising out of the commitment to focus on the situation of the conversion narrative is to attend closely to the interaction between the interviewer and the respondent. One cannot assume, as social scientists so often have done, that the observer's presence can be factored out of the situation. The respondent knows that the social scientist is there, the respondent will necessarily react to her, and the situation will be shaped by those reactions. In this sense interviews are, in Eliot Mishler's (1986b: 96) terms, "jointly produced discourses."

Another important implication of the presence of the interviewer is the role of what in psychoanalysis are called transference processes (Freud 1952, Devereux 1967, Crapanzano 1981). Both interviewer and respondent are likely to make assumptions about one another based on their emotional states and past experiences, and these assumptions can be one of the most revealing sources of information about the subject.

Fourth, in accordance with the principle that what is most important is what people do in social situations, the form of narrative analysis practiced here will attend most closely to the details of narrative style (Bakhtin 1981). This leads to a somewhat different approach to the role of narrative in the construction of identity than that which is prominent in the current literature in anthropology, sociology, and social psychology. There is by now a great deal of work that looks at the role narratives may play in the organization of self-conception.[3] While this is important work, it differs from the current analysis in its focus on self-conception, the (usually conscious) symbolizations of self that are formed by social actors. As explained above, in the current work I wish to focus on the relationship between self-conception and identity, a style of acting that may or may not be part of the conscious awareness of the actor. Such an approach necessitates attending less to narrative coherence than to the linguistic practices that allow actors to integrate disruptive conflicts in aims into an overarching canonical (Rappaport 1977) language (here, Evangelical Christianity). Thus my attention will be directed less toward the overall structure of the narratives that believers relate than to consistencies in the style of those narratives.

Although there is a well-developed tradition of the analysis of style in literature, in which narratives are examined in excruciating detail, such an approach is rarely applied in the analysis of narratives that are not considered "art," presumably on the self-perpetuating assumption that since such narratives are not art, they are insufficiently complex to provide a basis for this sort of analysis.

In contrast to conventional approaches, in examining the style of conversion narratives I hope to call attention to the art of these narratives, manifested above all in the style in which they are related. Although the language of these stories does not conform to the conventions of "literature," they may in fact be similar to works of literature in their patterned complexity. Thus it is appropriate to bring to bear on these narratives the sort of scrutiny Robert Alter (1981: 12) refers to as "literary analysis":

By literary analysis I mean the manifold varieties of minutely discriminating attention to the artful use of language, to the shifting play of ideas, conventions, tone, sound, imagery, syntax, narrative viewpoint, compositional units, and much else.

In order to depict the style of these narratives in a written medium, throughout the book I have used conventions for the transcription of speech that have been developed in the related fields of discourse analysis and conversational analysis. These conventions, which for the most part follow the system suggested by Moerman (1988), are recorded at the front of the book. Although these methods grow out of an attempt to accurately record as much of an utterance as is practically possible, it should not be imagined that I make any claim to record the speech of my consultants exactly. Anyone who has done this sort of work knows that there are considerable "judgment calls" involved in making a careful transcription.[4]

It may at times seem to the reader that speech is transcribed in unnecessary detail in this book. Many features of speech are transcribed, for example, that are not subsequently utilized in the analysis. Nevertheless, I think it important to transcribe what my consultants actually said with as much accuracy as possible. Conventional methods of transcribing speech reflect common-sense notions, and factor out as irrelevant signals such as pause length, stutters, voice tone, etc. In this way, conventional transcribing methods serve as a device for preserving the fiction that speakers have coherent intentions (cf. Mishler 1991; Ochs 1979).

That is, if I transcribe speech according to the conventions that are usually used, I will select what to transcribe and what to leave out largely on the basis of how I understand the speaker's intentions. If the speaker produces sounds that do not fit with my theory of his or her intentions, I will probably leave those sounds out of the transcription. They will be considered mere distractions from "the point." (And in fact if one starts to try to produce accurate transcriptions one will be faced with the criticism that one's transcriptions are distracting. This in spite of the idea that a transcription, by its nature, should be an empirical account of speech.)

Conventional transcription methods, then, reflect the referential linguistic ideology that plays a central role in sustaining a particular view of the subject in our society. In an attempt to work outside that ideology, it is necessary to – as much as is possible – not perpetuate its premises. It is in service of this aim that I have chosen to use transcription methods that do not factor out much of speech.

Jean: A fraternal twin

My first subject is a woman I will call Jean, a 35-year-old native English speaker of Philippine descent. My argument will be that the central concerns cited by Jean as leading up to the conversion event also manifest themselves in stylistic features of the conversion narrative. Furthermore, these stylistic features provide strong evidence that the conflict in aims that presumably animated the original conversion event continues to be present in the narrative itself. This demonstrates that this conflict was not resolved once and for all in the original conversion experience, but rather persists in the present. Jean thus uses the language of Evangelical Christianity not just as a means of reporting a past event, but also as a continuing means of articulating and presumably coming to terms with persisting ambivalence.

I turn now to the conversion narrative. The interview that I conducted with Jean took place in her home and lasted for about one hour. I had met her at a church where I was doing participant observation research, and she had immediately agreed to an interview. My interaction with her prior to the interview had been superficial and had taken place in the midst of larger groups.

Jean's conversion occurred, according to her account, in this way: shortly after leaving home to attend college, Jean heard a talk given by a Christian who had stressed the importance of "asking Christ into your life." Although she had been raised as a Roman Catholic, this was the first time Jean had heard that this might be considered a necessary part of being a Christian. She says that she regarded the speaker as "foolish," yet she found herself thinking about what he had said often over the next several weeks.

At this time Jean had begun to practice meditation, and had gotten into the habit of meditating under a particular tree on the college campus. One day, while meditating under the tree, Jean thought again of the speech she had heard, and decided to act on the advice she had received, to "ask

Christ into her life." She prayed and "nothing happened." Gradually, however, (over a period of several days) she began to feel that she was communicating with "the creator":

```
INTERVIEWER: um hm.........'h and-.......so
that-.....between thos:e.......those two ti:mes sitting
under the tree..........|you|
JEAN: |um hm|
INTERVIEWER: started to feel as though ................not          (5)
only that you COULD talk to the creator but that you were
talking to the creator....you- # in some sense sorta
communicated # with him |(you)|
JEAN: |YES| I felt like yes: it was possible to communicate
a:nd so: I did my thing about asking Christ into my          (10)
life..............and I did......BUT NO::THING,.........it
was just a slow realization that there was a
connection.........ma:de ((dec)).......but that was
it................
INTERVIEWER: uh huh                                                  (15)
JEAN: THAT was the only connection.........'h nothing
dramatic ha:ppened of course.....u:m...............I wasn't
expecting anything...............but I had a sense of
relief: tha:t..............that...........u:m.......I was
connected....I felt connected......some spiritual          (20)
forc:e...............was |behind me|
INTERVIEWER: |connected|.......connected
to::,..........|the creator|
JEAN: |(wha-) the crea::tor|
INTERVIEWER: |uh huh|                                               (25)
JEAN: |yes:| some connection.....som::e...................
INTERVIEWER: you say you felt relie::ved.........that you
were......|connected|
JEAN: |the = right|.....one of the reasons I was in....to
tra:nscendental meditation was                              (30)
to:.....'h.................LIKE I SAY.....uh communicate
with the tree: I wanted to learn about life.....'h I
wanted....to be INTEGRATED inta life..............I wanted
to be|
INTERVIEWER: |{um hm}|
JEAN:.......integrated inta just......life itself ((dec))           (35)
```

A striking feature of Jean's description of her conversion is the repeated use of various forms of the words "communicate" and, in particular, "connect." The latter term recurs five times in this section. It is worth noting that pauses at lines 19 and 26 strongly suggest that here Jean is trying to express the idea of connection in other terms, but is unable to do so to her satisfaction, for she returns to "connection." Finally, at line 33, she hits upon an alternative phrasing of this idea, using the word "integrated." "Communication," of course, can also be thought of as a variant on the theme of connection, referring as it does to close and effective interaction.

In light of the importance of "connection" in Jean's description of her conversion experience, it is significant that her discussions of her family are marked by a stress on a terminological family (Burke 1970) related to "disconnection." These passages are, from a rhetorical perspective, the inversion of the ones in which Jean discusses her conversion. Whereas there she placed great stress on her connection to the creator, here she stresses her disconnection from her family (primarily using the words "different" and "detached").

Jean has one sibling, a twin brother. In the following passages, note Jean's repeated stress on forms of the word "different" as she discusses her brother and herself. Note also a recurring parapraxis (slip of the tongue) as she tells the story of how she and her brother converted, simultaneously, to Christianity. Here is a portion of Jean's description of her brother:

INTERVIEWER: so: uh- so you look ba:ck and you try to think
of an ear:ly memory: or:.....................or something
and (#you think there's#) just not a whole lot <u>there</u>:? huh?
JEAN: 'H I s: u:m SO:ME but it's interesting my
<u>brother-</u>......and I ha:ve lived in the same house same   (40)
environment same parents?........'h and <u>he</u>? has totally
different perspective (than) I do.........fact my |bro|
INTERVIEWER: |{{huh}}|
JEAN: ther and I are very diff:erent

Jean goes on to answer my question about early memories, and then returns to the topic of her brother:

JEAN: and we're <u>very</u> different and   (45)
u:m..............he's..........I hate to <u>say</u>: this I mean
he's <u>still</u>: a hippie I mean |like|
INTERVIEWER: |ha|
JEAN: |he <u>still</u>| he has <u>always</u> had longer hair than I do #at
I mean#it's down to here......u:m.........I'VE been more   (50)
academic oriented
((some text omitted))
u::m..........(but) he's <u>just different</u> than I am,
I'M....the OPPOSITE u::m......u:m......I like a lot of
a:ction.......|and I like|
INTERVIEWER: |yeah| (55)
JEAN: a lot of movement..............
INTERVIEWER: uh huh

JEAN: an::d. . . . . .like I say, we're. . . .real
diff:erent. . . .I like. . . .business. . . .I like to
wheel and deal and. . . . .   (60)
INTERVIEWER: uh huh. . . . .|an:d|
JEAN: |and| he wouldn't care less:. . . .HE'LL |JUST PAY|
INTERVIEWER: |right|
JEAN: retail: I would never pay retail (ha)
INTERVIEWER: |(ha)| (65)
JEAN: |(ha)| I HAVE TO |(ha)|
INTERVIEWER: |uh huh uh huh|. . . . . .I see
JEAN: 'h AND ACTUALLY that's HOW we- an it's REAL
interesting because we did become Christians about the same
time. . . . . .'h through different different or- different   (70)
organizations. . . . . . .
INTERVIEWER: uh huh
JEAN: 'H an:d we've always known that we were s-
diff:erent. . . . . . .and we- even though we're twins, we've
always had separate li- very se:parate lives |just| (75)
INTERVIEWER: |uh huh|
JEAN: you know. . . .'h and it was only when we became a
Christian that we beca:me. . . . . . .really tight

In these few lines of text, Jean explicitly asserts that she is "different"
from or "opposite" to her brother a total of seven times (at lines 42, 44, 45,
52, 53, 59, 74), in addition to emphasizing that she and her brother have
had "very separate" lives and that they converted to Christianity through
different (repeated three times) organizations. At lines 77–78 there occurs
an example of the other notable feature of Jean's discussion of her
brother, parapraxes in which she refers to herself and her brother as a
single unit ("when we became a Christian").[5] These parapraxes are what I
have labeled (following Labov and Fanshel 1977: 46) "deniable communications": they are examples of speech acts through which messages can be
conveyed without the speaker taking full responsibility for them. There
are three more such slips in a period of under three minutes while Jean
discusses her brother. The first indicates some confusion about how she
should refer to her brother's age:

JEAN: ((some text omitted)) kind of like an: office clerk
when he was #we were about-# #he was about# seven- sixteen   (80)
or seventeen

The second parapraxis echoes the one that occurs at lines 78–79:

JEAN: ((some text omitted)) and how we became a Christian
simultaneously WITHOUT KNOWING the other one was becoming a
INTERVIEWER: uh huh
JEAN: Christian too   (85)

In the third parapraxis, Jean refers to herself and her brother as "I" and then corrects the error (line 96):

INTERVIEWER: so that.........then when-.......when you were
growing up do you remember like fi:ghting with your brother
or:
JEAN: YEAH well yeah..............but I mean you know like
I guess its just kid's stuff I mean nothing:....dramatic   (90)
INTERVIEWER: {uh huh}
JEAN: 'h we were just....we just sort of knew we were
different.......he had |his set of|
INTERVIEWER: |{{uh huh}}|
JEAN: friends and I had my set of friends.........I: went   (95)
to- we went to different schoo:ls and I went to a
mor:e...........academic
INTERVIEWER: uh huh.....
JEAN: a college prep-......s:chool

These slips, of course, belie Jean's explicit statements that she and her brother are very different. In fact, the recurrent communication (Labov and Fanshel 1977) that this difference is significant is itself an example of the most basic of rhetorical devices: one seeks to convince by repeating. Jean's stress on her difference from her brother, in other words, can be taken as evidence that she needs to convince someone of that difference. The passage quoted thus illustrates Jean's ambivalence around the issue of her connection or attachment to her brother: although she overtly asserts her separation and distance from him, she uses deniable channels of communication to convey her sense of unity with him.

It is possible that Jean's concern with her degree of separation from her brother is related to the fact that he is her twin. Clinicians I have consulted on this issue have told me that it is not uncommon for twins to manifest conflicts over boundary issues.[6] The theoretical reasoning behind this observation is most easily explained from the standpoint of ego psychology: If one makes the assumption that every infant faces the developmental task of forging a separate self out of an initial state of symbiosis with the mother (Mahler, Pine, and Bergman 1975), then one can see how twins might face a particularly complex version of this task. As psychoanalyst Marjorie Leonard (1961: 307) has written:

In the case of twins, each infant not only must go through this same process of becoming aware of himself as separate from his mother, and the ensuing primary identification with her, but he has an additional task, that of separating himself from his twin ... To the infant, everything outside of himself is an extension of himself, until through frustration he perceives the separation. Therefore, to the extent to which one twin is aware of the existence of the other in the first weeks of infancy, there must be a sense of oneness, or rather a lack of perception of separateness.

Leonard goes on to cite evidence – for the most part of an anecdotal, clinical nature – that these early developmental complications often persist as some form of boundary confusion in later life:

The influence of the primary intertwin identification is similarly evident in later stages of development, in some instances throughout the life of the twins. This identification with the twin often retards the maturation of both individuals, causing language difficulties and interfering with the formation of other object relationships. Just as the dependency on the mother prevents complete separation of the maternal and self-images in the single child, the dependency of one twin on the other often causes their self-images to remain blurred. (1961: 309)

Although Leonard surely overgeneralizes here in her evaluation of the likelihood of maturational problems among twins, her observations coincide with those of other clinicians I have consulted. Of course, it is not possible to trace the etiology of Jean's concern with her separation from her brother, but the evidence presented here clearly demonstrates that such concern exists. This concern with separation is not limited, however, to Jean's discussion of her relationship with her brother; it can be further documented in Jean's discussion of her relationship with her parents, where it is couched in terms of detachment and attachment. Again I quote a key section of the interview:

```
INTERVIEWER: can you tell: me anything                                    (100)
about...........................I-I guess I don't have
much sense yet of.................of what your fa:ther or
mother would- were were like as people......or....around the
hous::e or..........u::m........how they came across to
you.....in this:....dis:tant....foggy (ha) |past| ((the last          (105)
four words are pronounced slowly and dramatically, to create
a sense of mock melodrama))
JEAN: 'H| WELL uh THEY: uh THEY: I FEEL VERY DETA-I'll
be honest with you I feel very detached........from them
INTERVIEWER: um hm?........and m-maybe you did even
the:n....
JEAN: yeah I still do                                                     (110)
INTERVIEWER: uh huh
JEAN: 'h a::nd #actually I'll be hones(t) with you # I've
always felt guil:ty:......of feeling that
deta::chment.............
INTERVIEWER: huh, ((descending tone))............uh           (115)
huh......
JEAN: and I don't know why I just do........I do NOT feel
close to them..........
```

INTERVIEWER: huh, an:d......pretty much never have
JEAN: 'h and I ALWAYS feel GUILTY I don't know WHY: I #feel   (120)
guilty about it but I feel guilty about it#........
INTERVIEWER: uh huh.......and that's kind of
a:.................I guess:..........something that's
been kind of sta:ble in your life you've never felt close to
them and you've always felt like you really kinda should but   (125)
JEAN: 'H yea:h and I do:n't and I'm just very different than
they are, they're very....fa- they u::m.......'h I
feel.....they-I th-it's almost like.....((dec)) they want me
to be atta:ched to them:........{and I'm no:t, and I feel   (130)
guilty because I'm not what they want me to
be}.......((voice wavering, dropping intonation))
INTERVIEWER: uh huh........u::m.......yes: well (ha) {{this
happens a lot with parents......you know they have
expectations}}   (135)
JEAN: um hm ((rising then falling tone))
INTERVIEWER: 'h u::m...................................
JEAN: ((sounds of weeping))
INTERVIEWER: o:kay ((descending tone))
JEAN: um hm? ((sharply rising tone))   (140)

The first comment I must make here concerns my role as interviewer,
and the relationship I forge with Jean during the interview. As noted, at
line 105 I conclude my question with an ironic tone, evidently in a manner
that makes light of Jean's inability to recall her own past. I was surprised
to hear this on the tape, for I do not remember doing this intentionally.
Therefore, I am in no better position than any other observer to say why
the question was posed in this way. However, the nature of my pauses
earlier in the question (at lines 101, 102, 104), indicates something I am
aware of, namely that Jean felt uncomfortable talking about her childhood and I felt uncomfortable asking about it. The long pauses occur as I
reformulate the question and fill time because I sense her resistance to
answering. This would suggest that I concluded the question as I did in
order to remove some of the tension from the situation, to take things in a
lighter direction.[7] As the overlap indicates, Jean signals her agreement to
speak in a transition that was clearly carefully orchestrated to avoid
further tension. However, she does not accept my invitation to reframe the
situation in a less serious manner (Goffman 1986). Rather, she plunges
ahead in a very emotional manner: the tension is relieved by her decision
to talk about what has been troubling her.

This eagerness to proceed is very evident at line 112, where Jean
breathes in audibly and draws out the appositional "and" in order to
assert her right to speak, evidently before she knows precisely what she
wants to say (see Sacks, Schegloff, and Jefferson 1974: 719). In the

following section, there are again signs that the interviewer is trying to tone down the emotional content of Jean's speech and that Jean is not willing to do this. I refer in particular to the interchange between lines 119 and 121, when I offer Jean the opportunity to retreat from her confession of guilt to a recapitulation of her feelings of distance from her parents. She ignores my offer and continues on the topic that is relevant to her at that moment, her feelings concerning her relationship with her parents.[8] The form of this interchange clearly testifies to its over-whelming emotional importance to Jean. Of course, the most striking evidence of that importance is the fact that Jean begins to weep, probably at line 131.

It follows that the topic of this section, Jean's detached relationship with her parents and her feelings of guilt about that relationship, are emotionally salient for her. As was the case in her discussion of her brother, her intense feelings center around the topic of separation. Here the primary word in the terminological family is detachment. The fact that Jean says she feels guilty about her lack of attachment to her parents can be taken as evidence that she feels substantial ambivalence about the issue of separation from her family.

To summarize, it has been shown that Jean's discussions of family and her religious experience are, from a rhetorical perspective, inversely related: whereas the idea of connection seems central to her religious life, it is important to her to assert "separation" in the context of her family. This assertion, however, is the site of considerable ambivalence.

Another way to state the latter point is that discussions of religion and family are also distinguished on the stylistic level. Her discussions of family contain considerable evidence of conflict: hesitations, demon-strated emotion that interferes with speech, overstress, and deniable communications contradicting her assertion of separation. These signs are noticeably absent in lines 1–35 above, describing her religious conversion. Her speech is more fluent here, in that it is less disrupted by pauses and reformulations. In fact, the only noticeable lapses of fluency occur as she struggles with the problem of reformulating the conception of connection; this is not a problem that is indicative of ambivalence. There are no obvious deniable communications here, and no noticeable interference of speech due to emotion.

The evidence of Jean's narration points clearly to the conclusion that while separation from her family is an emotion-charged issue marked by a conflict in aims (the simultaneous desire for connection and separation), connection to the divinity can be asserted without interference. This observation is significant, of course, in light of the fact that Jean describes her conversion as a connection. Jean's ability to feel connection to the divinity is an experience that organizes her entire biography; it is the turning point of her life. The evidence presented here substantiates the interpretation that a feeling of connection has this overwhelming importance because it somehow enables Jean to come to terms with her conflict about separation and connection. A further examination of Jean's story will help to clarify how this happens.

Jean's integration into a community of men

Jean's ambivalent feelings about connection and separation can be observed in many aspects of her interview. For example, she describes a work history that is in general successful, but marked by considerable fluctuations. Jean has a history of throwing herself into different careers, pursuing them very successfully, but eventually having to give them up because she has, on her account, depleted her energy. Thus several years of ascent within an organization will be followed by a period of inactivity or even of hospitalization due to exhaustion. Jean's work history, then, further exemplifies the theme of difficulty with connection and separation.

Another instructive example here is a series of episodes Jean describes that took place several years before the interview. These episodes have to do with her involvement, both in work and in her religious life, with groups of gay men. This involvement, which took place subsequent to her conversion, is not discussed in explicitly religious terms. However, Jean's experience in this community highlights certain of the themes I want to develop about Jean's concerns about intimacy, and so I shall spend some time looking at her discussion of this topic.

Jean explains that she had a job in the fashion industry which brought her into contact with a large group of gay men:

INTERVIEWER: |uh huh|
JEAN: |and| (ha) #I frea:ked out because I couldn't find any
job#.....'h so the:n......'h #I PRAYED and prayed about it
and nothing had ha:ppened ((speech slightly slurred)) and
then all of a sudden I got this#....jo::b, ((marked   (145)
descending tone)).......uh working in *fashion*
advertising.......with....|forty|
INTERVIEWER: |huh|
JEAN: ....homosexuals (ha) ((laughs while saying
homosexuals))

Jean immediately goes on to discuss her relationship with this group of men:

JEAN: and I was like a den: mother,.... ((voice change;   (150)
spoken like an aside))

INTERVIEWER: uh huh. . . . . .you- you- so- you- were you
the only woman?
JEAN: ye:s (ha)
INTERVIEWER: wow ((descending tone))
JEAN: a:nd. . . .when:. . . .(and) I::(m). . . .very- I got very   (155)
close to these me:n and at that time. . . . . . .'h gay men were
no:t. . . . . .IT was still a clos:et situation |here|
INTERVIEWER: |uh huh|
JEAN: it wasn't. . . . . . .u:m. . . . . .u:m. . . . . . .people
weren't tha:t. . . .verbal about it, |#or that open about it,#| (160)
INTERVIEWER: |uh huh uh huh|. . . .uh huh
JEAN: a:nd um. . . . .'h they were VE:RY afrai?::d, ((voice
change; smile voice)) and they tell me- uh they #told me
about this# later o:n. . . . . .'h they were very? afraid that if   (165)
I found? out. . . .what they were all: about (ha)
INTERVIEWER: uh huh. . . . . . .
JEAN: that I would qui:t, |and|
INTERVIEWER: |{uh huh}|
JEAN: they really liked, me   (170)
INTERVIEWER: {uh huh}
JEAN: a:nd. . . . .((end smile voice)) I KNE:W?
INTERVIEWER: |{uh huh}|
JEAN: |I| DON'T KNOW WHY: but I HAD a #genuine love for them
((speech slurred)) and I really liked them and I wanted to   (175)
be: with them # ((volume decreasing, spoken with emphasis))

One noticeable feature of this passage is that the aside and voice change
at line 150 (together with similar features in the passages below) contri-
bute to a more histrionic style of story-telling than is typical of Jean's
speech in the interview as a whole. It is possible that she is unintentionally
mimicking the style of her previous interaction with these men as she
speaks in the present. That is, although this observation opens me to the
charge of stereotyping, it is nevertheless true that communities of gay men
sometimes incorporate and elaborate histrionic speaking styles, and it is
possible that Jean's speech may reflect such a style here. The slip on tense
at line 164, which is a common error in Jean's speech, could also be used to
support the interpretation that Jean is sufficiently caught up in the story to
in some ways recapitulate these past events in the present.

On the level of content, one cannot miss the familial idiom in which
Jean discusses her relationship with these men. In the first place, of course,
she refers to her relationship with them as being like that of a den mother.
But there are other important clues here as well which point to the
conclusion that Jean conceives of this situation as a family. The gay men
are spoken of in the aggregate; their sexual orientation evidently renders
them a community in a way that would not exist among forty heterosexual

men. They have emotions in common; at lines 165–66 we learn that they were all very afraid of Jean's judgment of them, and at line 170 that they all liked her. In the weakest interpretation we can say that Jean regards the men as a close-knit community, reminiscent of a family. In a stronger interpretation, the men are her children, a vulnerable group who had had no mother to protect them.

The final evidence of the familial salience of this group for Jean is of course the emergence of what could be called the thematic metaphor of Jean's narrative, the issue of intimacy. The men liked Jean, she liked them, loved them, and – for reasons she says she does not understand – wanted to be with them.

As could by now be predicted, however, the issue of intimacy provokes contradiction and ambivalence. As Jean continues to reconstruct her relationship to this group of men, she arrives at the issue which eventually separated her from them:

```
JEAN: but uh..............I: after two suic- I: had, #I got
real close to some of them # and a lot of
them..........{felt-close to
me,}........a:nd...........u:m these #are on #                (180)
different....occasions but........u:m.............I got
rea:lly....close to:....one of the lovers of the guys
INTERVIEWER: uh huh
JEAN: that |that|
INTERVIEWER: |uh huh|                                        (185)
JEAN: I worked with.......a:nd he was very
depress:ed.....|that|
INTERVIEWER: |{uh huh}|
JEAN: {{they had broken up}}
INTERVIEWER: uh huh |uh huh|                                 (190)
JEAN: |we had| #talked and talked and talked#..........A:ND
just before he:......committed suicide {he}
INTERVIEWER: {uh huh}..........
JEAN: I sa:w him
INTERVIEWER: uh huh                                          (195)
JEAN: I didn't know he was that close to suicide, but
INTERVIEWER: uh huh
JEAN: he called me and wanted me to come over and,
((decreasing volume)).......have tea with him
INTERVIEWER: uh huh, uh huh                                  (200)
JEAN: a:nd appa:rently:,.......at the funera:l, uh: he spoke
highly of me:....among ....his.........|men and|
INTERVIEWER: |uh huh|
JEAN: women friends
INTERVIEWER: uh huh                                          (205)
JEAN: I HARDLY knew this guy::,
```

INTERVIEWER: {hm}

JEAN: #I mean I REALLY did not know this guy at all, I mean #.....'h #I was nice to him, (and) I talked to him, and #......encouraged him   (210)

INTERVIEWER: {uh huh}

JEAN: but the wa:y he:...........TALKED ABOUT ME: among his friends,

INTERVIEWER: uh huh?

JEAN: he-.........ma:de them feel like I was #VERY VERY   (215)
close to him?#

INTERVIEWER: uh huh

JEAN: a:nd I was his best frie:nd, and I was............he:..........he FELT real close,........

INTERVIEWER: uh huh   (220)

JEAN: but I: KNE:W that I wasn't that close to him ((volume decreases)).......AND I FELT really sick insi:de that....here i- here was this man who was VERY lonely and VERY typical of the......the men that were there.....'H ALL: fla:sh,......#lots of dancing, lots of parties, lots of   (225)
clubs, # ((indistinguishable))

INTERVIEWER: uh huh

JEAN: BUT UH INsi:de VE:RY very lonely,

INTERVIEWER: uh huh

JEAN: an:d....if they thought I was close to them,....and I   (230)
knew I wasn't, I mean,....((speech slows)) the:y had no idea what intimacy was all about

INTERVIEWER: uh huh

JEAN: and uh.................I felt sick   (235)
insi:de..........and then also felt.....sicker when (ha) #I (found out) I was the last person to see him alive# ((volume decreases)).............

INTERVIEWER: uh huh

At line 201, there is a "he" with an ambiguous referent. This line makes sense only if it assumed that the person referred to here was not someone at the funeral, but rather the man who committed suicide. In that case, this phrase does not, as it initially appears to do, describe what he said at the funeral, for people do not generally speak at their own funerals. That is, Jean says here, to paraphrase, "at the funeral I learned that this man (the man who committed suicide) had spoken highly of me to his friends." Thus this passage contains a striking self-contradiction. At lines 181–182 Jean tells us that she "got very close" to the man who eventually committed suicide, and at line 191 she stresses how much they talked to one another. However, at lines 206–221 she repeatedly denies having been close to this man, asserting that she "hardly knew" him, wasn't close to him at all, and so on. Here, then, is some very powerful evidence of Jean's confusion and ambivalence about the issue of intimacy.

Given this confusion, lines 231–232 can be read as not only about the gay men, but about Jean herself. It is not only they who don't know what intimacy is about, it is Jean as well. This impression is further strengthened if one examines Jean's account of the second suicide. Here she is describing her involvement in a group of homosexual Christians:

```
JEAN: #THEY HAD HETEROsexuals in the group too,# 'h                    (240)
INTERVIEWER: uh huh
JEAN: but I: wa:s....part of this group and I
felt..............so:
u::m........whe:n?........this.....GUY committed suicide
u:m.......................it really affected a lot of the                (245)
peopl:e in- the ch- the Christian ((name deleted))
group....|#Christian homosexual|
INTERVIEWER: |uh huh|
JEAN: group or whatever they call it# =
INTERVIEWER: =they had known, him......                                 (250)
JEAN: 'h no #they didn't know im# but they knew that I was
struggling....o:ver this
INTERVIEWER: uh huh uh huh
JEAN: and they frea:ked? out because they knew that
it....((voice change, intentionally deep voice)) could                   (255)
have been them: ((dec))..........
INTERVIEWER: uh huh
JEAN: if they didn't become a Christian,
INTERVIEWER: uh huh
JEAN: and that we have to really draw....'h more strength                (260)
from Christ,
((some text omitted))
JEAN: a:nd I: think I accomplished that,.........what
HAPPENED later on? was that uh....I had another friend
and....this guy I was-....pretty close to, I really
liked him a lot, and {he was a little screwed up}                        (265)
and........his psychiatrist {used to call me all the ti:me,
and we'd....you kno:w....keep no:tes on (which)- |how|
INTERVIEWER: |hm|
JEAN: (ha) George was doing}....... 'h a:nd George
u::m...........((clicking sound))'h also committed suicide               (270)
(ha)......
INTERVIEWER: {oh}
JEAN: a:nd....they never found his body,....but....they
kno:w that he ((identifying reference deleted))
INTERVIEWER: uh huh                                                      (275)
JEAN: and u:m............................I think? it was
at tha:t time- at tha:t point that I just knew I had to
```

leave {I couldn't take it any mo:re.....I couldn't stand the
fact that people were killing themselves, it was
just-}.......'h.........I w- I wanted to gi:ve but I felt   (280)
that all my energy {was already}............
INTERVIEWER: uh huh
JEAN: {deple:ted},....
INTERVIEWER: uh huh
JEAN: and I didn't know how to ha:ndle it.....   (285)
INTERVIEWER: uh huh.....
JEAN: it was like I wanted to give and I {couldn't give
cause I didn't have anything to give}....|and I think|
INTERVIEWER: |uh huh|
JEAN: that's when.......there are times when you have to   (290)
s:top your work and just rest,
((some text omitted))
INTERVIEWER: uh huh,......................and-......but
these- these suicide situations obviously really |affected|
JEAN: |I:-|
INTERVIEWER: you tremendously   (295)
JEAN: #I didn't know how to handle that,#
INTERVIEWER: uh huh...................................
JEAN: I've never been that....{close to death}
INTERVIEWER: uh huh................|uh huh|
JEAN: |I think| what it was was the:.............the   (300)
lo:neliness that {they, felt?.............frightened me}
#because they really felt? tha:t#...........and I
couldn't...........I couldn't....fulfi:ll
tha:t......nee:d,...........{for them}

At lines 255–256, Jean says that her friend's suicide was troubling to the
members of the Christian group because they knew they could have taken
their lives as well. Again, I read this as a statement about Jean at the same
time as it is a statement about the members of the group. The suicide
scared her because she knows it could have been her, that the emptiness
driving her friends towards self-destruction was something she herself felt.
This emerges clearly at lines 276–291, where Jean explains that the second
suicide drove her away from these men. They had taken so much of her
energy that she herself was in danger of being "depleted." As is the case
throughout the interview, this feeling is not only described but re-enacted
in these lines. Beginning at line 278 Jean's voice grows noticeably weaker;
she is depleted as she describes having one time been in that state. One can
glimpse here the nature of the feelings that have caused such fluctuations
in her work career, for she says that it is these sorts of feelings that mean
one must stop one's work and just rest. Thus this situation can be linked to
a broader theme in the interview – Jean's tendency to throw herself into a
context, become very involved, and eventually to feel that the context

poses a threat to her existence. In the passage above, the nature of that threat becomes clear: it is the possibility of oblivion through depletion of Jean's sense of her own resources.

Further insight into the nature of these theatening feelings can be gained by attending to the end of this passage. Here Jean confesses that she was frightened by a loneliness that she could not overcome; her own personal reserves were threatened by the demands being made on her by others. The ultimate consequence of these demands is made clear at lines 297–298. Here Jean, obviously moved in light of a pause that lasts 3.7 seconds, names the threat as the proximity of death.

The section on Jean's relationship with the gay men, then, clarifies and strengthens a number of points I have made earlier. First, Jean is drawn towards intense involvement in familial situations because of the possibility of intimacy that such situations provide. However, she typically finds that her involvement in the situation somehow escapes her control, so that she faces the possibility that the demands that the situation makes on her threaten her with oblivion. It is this dilemma that could be said to constitute her ambivalence about connection: the more she gives, the more vulnerable she is to others taking too much. Eventually, the conflict can be resolved in only one way, through fleeing the situation.

Connection and excommunication

This theme can also be located in the stories that Jean tells about her ongoing religious life. Here the problem of connection and separation is particularly acute, because here two forms of connection are juxtaposed, her connection to the religious group and her connection to God.

Jean cries twice during the interview; first, as has been shown, in her discussion of her feelings of guilt about her lack of connection to her family. The second time she cries occurs when she describes her excommunication from a small and tightly knit "house church" she joined some time after her conversion. (Such churches are small groups of "true believers" who meet in members' homes. Note, then, their family-like characteristics.) Jean had been living with a man outside of marriage, a situation her fellow church members could not accept. A representative group of church members came to see her at her house and tried to convince her to repent. They told her she was living a life of sin, and Jean responded that if they felt that way they should remove her from the church rolls:

JEAN: if you feel that way....just....take me off......'h   (305)
a:nd then they started tellin me abou:t ho:w.........'h
u::m............tha:t I was living the r: u:h

living::.........a LIFE..................of <u>sin</u>,
((pronounced tone drop)) and I was on the road to <u>death</u>,
((pronounced tone drop)) and af I sh if I <u>hang</u> out with   (310)
these people any <u>longer</u> you know it was gonna be <u>all over</u>
and there was no <u>stop:ping</u> and........((rhythmic, almost sing-song prosody))
INTERVIEWER: uh huh
JEAN: 'h u::m......basi<u>cal</u>ly they (ha) <u>ex</u>communicated me
((laughing begins at "excommunicated"))
INTERVIEWER: uh huh uh huh.......   (315)
JEAN: uh- IN OTHER WORDS they were WASHING their
hands.....WASHING their hands⁹ and saying
'h.............you choo:se that life ((dec)) we're WARNING
<u>you</u>: if you DON'T con-if you DON'T........repen:t and you
DON'T conform to our wa:ys.......<u>you</u> know....it's death all   (320)
the way
INTERVIEWER: uh huh
JEAN: blablabla....'h..........a:nd I kept saying well- <u>go</u>
<u>ahead</u> and leave me:........a:nd....<u>they?</u> didnt really wanna
take any responsibility of me.....   (325)
INTERVIEWER: uh huh |uh huh|
JEAN: |ei:ther| so they e- I got excommunicated,
INTERVIEWER: uh huh, |{yeah},|
JEAN: |SO:| CONSEQUENTLY I didn't go to church
for........<u>I::</u> ((spoken very loudly)) was REA::LLY......I   (330)
MEAN ((very loud)) #I WASNT really going to church ANYway? I mean I
was going every <u>now</u> and <u>then</u>.....'h bu:t BY THAT TIME I was <u>TOALLY</u>
TURNED OFF: by the church ((dec, dropping tone, speech slightly slurred))
INTERVIEWER: uh huh
JEAN: JU:ST......   (335)
INTERVIEWER: uh huh
JEAN: <u>turned off</u>
INTERVIEWER: uh huh..............
JEAN: and:
uh-.......u::m....................................<u>really</u>   (340)
.....mixed up too cause................((dec, growing
softer)) I really thought it was {all
over}.............with- wiih God...........
INTERVIEWER: uh huh
JEAN: 'H I really <u>thou::ght</u> ((slowly))........that <u>Go:d</u>   (345)
((voice breaks)) had excommunicated me ((very
slowly)).......
INTERVIEWER: SO....in a sense.........you <u>belie:ved</u> what
they:....had.....((dec)) 'h
JEAN: yeah? ((pronounced rising tone)).......
INTERVIEWER: {had to:ld you}   (350)
JEAN: 'h I <u>still</u> feel very <u>hurt</u>....about it ((voice breaking, weeping))........
INTERVIEWER: uh huh

This episode establishes beyond any doubt that the issue of connection is of central emotional importance for Jean. Her conversion establishes a sense of connection to God, and the "excommunication" is, on a rhetorical level, the most painful way imaginable for her fellow church members to ask her to leave their group. It is painful because it is a severing of her connection to God, a return to separation. The spectre of being unable to express her connection to God causes Jean to break down in tears.

Canonical language and contradicting aims

The underlying issue in this interview is best conceived as a problem of contradictory aims. Jean is simultaneously attracted to the intimacy entailed in close family (and family-like) relations and compelled to break free of the restrictions entailed in such relations. The depth of each of these desires is evidenced in the interview. To be uninvolved in intimate relationships is to feel the sort of loneliness she recognized among the gay men. Yet to be involved in such relationships is to be subject to depletion, and perhaps also to engulfment. Both are unbearable; time after time Jean simply has to leave the situations where she has temporarily found the intimacy with others that she seeks.

Becoming immersed in and then leaving social relationships is the story of Jean's life. Jean has spent her adult life throwing herself into a series of careers which she subsequently abandons; she also has a history of romantic relationships that last for relatively short periods of time. And of course, Jean's ambivalence about separation is manifested when she joins a house church with stringent rules, and then proceeds to undertake an activity which she must know will precipitate her expulsion from the group.

All of these behaviors manifest the enduring conflict between two contradictory aims of intimacy and freedom from the demands of others. And Jean herself recognizes that even her commitment to a religious group will eventually bring her to face this conflict. She says, of her involvement in the house church:

JEAN: a:nd u:m. . . . . .I just wanted some
real. . . . . .basic. . . . . . . .guidelines. . . . . . .'h. . . .and u:m   (355)
. . . . .I STARTED TO REALIZE that
per<u>hap</u>s the chu:rch became maybe like. . . . .<u>my:</u> situation with
the- my <u>par</u>ents. . . . .'h you just sorta <u>fol:</u>low the
<u>ru:</u>les. . . . .and you don't ask <u>quest</u>ions. . . .you kno:w like #I
was a pretty obedient # child 'h. . . . . . .   (360)

It is only in one context that Jean is truly free to express her need for connection with no corresponding threat to her own sense of boundaries. As is clear from her speech behavior, she is able to assert a connection to God without such evidence of ambivalence. This suggests that Jean's use of religious language provides her with the emotional resources of "connection" without threatening to overwhelm her though stringent rules, demands for too much closeness, or (perhaps) a psychological merger with her twin.

Jean's conversion narrative provides clear evidence of the use of the language of Evangelical Christianity to express an aim that is frustrated in other social contexts. Jean's ambivalence has not disappeared as a result of her conversion; that is surely evident from the style of her narration. What has happened, rather, is that through the use of a canonical language she can assert her needs for connection and separation simultaneously. Because of the Christian rhetoric of communion with God in all its forms, Jean can conceive herself as connected to God. But her desire for distance is also expressed in her relationship to the divine, for God has no troubling needs of his own that must be met.

Thus my claims here extend beyond the argument that the family situation is the emotional paradigm for Jean's religious concerns.[10] My concern here is rather with the transformation of intention. From this perspective, an identity that coincides poorly with an actor's self-conception is equivalent to the communicating of multiple and contradictory purposes. The person who acts in this way will engage in behaviors that in our society will be construed as "meaningless," behaviors that cannot be sorted out socially to adumbrate a coherent position. It was of course Freud's greatest intuition to see that much of what had been dismissed as meaningless – the dream, the slip of the tongue, the paralyzed arm – was in fact communication.[11] I depart from his general perspective only to the extent that I (as do many contemporary psychoanalysts) resist the conclusion that such communications reflect conflicts in the structure of the personality. Rather, I regard this idea of structural conflict as simply a reification of the ability of people to produce ambiguous communications.

What may be observed very clearly in Jean's conversion narrative is the way in which the meaningless becomes precisely the basis for that which is most meaningful, her sense of connection. The feelings that produce speech difficulties in the context of her family, difficulties that may be assumed to represent significant ambivalence in Jean's aims, are at the same time the basis for her connection to God, a connection that is absolutely central to how she understands her place in the world. In this transition between the meaningless and the meaningful, a commitment is formed. Jean is committed to Christianity because she has found something meaningful there in her connection to God. At the same time, she has found a context – perhaps the only context – in which her needs for closeness can be expressed with no corresponding fear of her being depleted or overwhelmed.

In terms of the language of the metaphoric and the canonical, Jean's conversion can be understood – and this is precisely how she herself explains it – as a grasping of the full impact of the canonical image of a "connection" to God. Jean uses this idea to draw within the boundaries of referential communication aims that previously had found expression only metaphorically in the broad sense of the term, that is, in uninterpretable communications that probably manifested themselves for the most part as disturbances in communication.

But this achievement was not a one-time event. It continues to occur now as Jean tells her story. Her ambivalent aims are invoked as she speaks of her family, yet the signs thereof disappear as she speaks of her relationship to God. What Jean presents as a moment of salvation is better conceived, from this perspective, as the discovery of a technique, a way of dealing with ambivalence that may be used again and again. The conversion narrative is a performance in which her conflicts manifest themselves and then are resolved through her use of the canonical language. As she struggles to explain what being a Christian means to her, she seeks after terms and concepts – such as the possibility of being close to God – that capture her feelings. This struggle can be conceived as the use of the canonical language to draw unacknowledged aims within the realm of the sayable.

It is as yet unclear, however, just how this transition from the meaningless to the meaningful occurs. It is surely important that Jean has learned to express an ambivalence in her relationship to God that she is forbidden to express in the context of her family. But what are the conditions necessary for a resolution of this type? Surely the process of moving between the realm of unacknowledged aims and their expression in religious language is not a simple matter of consciously intending such a transition, for the unacknowledged aim is itself by definition outside of awareness. What are the preconditions that set up the possibility for such a shift between the metaphoric and the canonical?

4   Dreams

I have suggested that the narrating of a conversion story may be seen as a ritual performance in which the narrator expresses and comes to terms with contradictory aims. The efficacy of this ritual in bringing about self-transformation may be traced to the fact that the narrative allows the believer to express unacknowledged purposes in a shared canonical language rather than in idiosyncratic behavior. Thus what have been construed as meaningless behaviors, behaviors that meshed poorly with the subject's self-conception, may be reintegrated into a system of meaning. In this chapter I want to examine in some detail the processes whereby first, an unacknowledged purpose is formulated in terms of a canonical language and second, canonical language may acquire a personal meaning for the believer.

Self-transformation and commitment

Referential communicative behaviors, as explained in the introduction, take place within the confines of the familiar, so that one can fairly speak of consensual interpretations being attached to these behaviors. In the realm of the referential, communicative symbols can be said to "stand for" something else, that something else being the consensual interpretation of the symbol. Within this realm, then, all utterances can be more or less accurately glossed in terms of other utterances; this property of language use is what makes dictionaries possible (Silverstein 1976: 15–16).

In our society referential functions of language use are highlighted and constitutive functions are masked. We are taught to attend to the creation of referential meaning as what we are doing; it is our intention. Constitutive activity, such as the "slip of the tongue," is not what we are doing, and is ignored as meaningless.

Thus it happens that some constitutive functions of language – specifically, those that I have labelled "metaphoric" – are, at least in this cultural context, often construed as non-intentional. I have argued, however, that it is more accurate to think of metaphoric constitutive activity as expressing unacknowledged purposes. In fact, even the term "expressing" here is misleading. A slip of the tongue is most accurately described not as expressing an unacknowledged purpose but rather as constituting, as *being* an unacknowledged purpose.

This formulation points to an approach to the central question of this book, that of the relationship between the two aspects of the conversion experience, self-transformation and increased commitment to the religious system. For what happens in many of the conversion narratives I have studied is that what I have called metaphoric communicative behaviors blend with the canonical language; the narrative may be seen as the site of the transition between unacknowledged purposes and the formulation of those purposes within the realm of the referential.

That is, it may happen that a believer comes to be able to formulate in terms of the canonical language an unacknowledged purpose, as Jean does when she expresses her desire for "connection" in terms of her relationship to God. What has previously taken shape as metaphoric activity may now take shape as religious activity; the constitutive is thereby drawn into the referential. An unacknowledged purpose that has until now been formulated as uninterpretable activity is now formulated in terms of the canonical language. An example of this process might be a healing experience, in which an emotion or conflict that has manifested itself in a physical symptom comes to be expressed in the believer's understanding of her relationship to God. Such a process is often experienced as self-transformation. The reason for this is that unacknowledged purposes manifest themselves as an identity – things a person does – that in some ways contradicts the person's self-conception. The possibility of formulating these purposes in the canonical language creates an opportunity to stop formulating them in involuntary behavior.

The conversion narrative may also involve a shift in the opposite direction, in which the referential is drawn into the constitutive. Aspects of the canonical language now come to acquire emotional depth as unacknowledged purposes are formulated in terms of these aspects of the language. This is the basis for increased commitment. This sort of movement is often evidenced in the "concrete" rhetoric of the conversion experience, which in the United States is often labeled with phrases such as "a personal encounter with Jesus Christ." That is, what has previously been understood strictly in terms of consensual associations comes to be felt as possessing an immense but inarticulable significance, as being metaphoric.

Jim: family background

Jim, who was introduced at the outset, is a fit and young-looking man in his early fifties. The first characteristic of Jim's style that should be noted is his "intellectual" approach to his religion and the interview; Jim construed his relationship to me as that of a fellow intellectual who shared an interest in religion. An articulate man, Jim is similar to the sort of person that many anthropologists have been delighted to use as "key informants." He has a deep appreciation for the symbolism of his culture and a tireless fascination with the task of interpreting this symbolism. Unlike some other key informants, however, Jim claims to speak not for any group but only for himself. It is the relevance of Christian symbolism to his personal situation which is the object of his interest.

Jim was born, the second of five children, in rural Minnesota. His father was a farmer and his mother a housewife. His mother was also an extremely religious woman, a member of a very conservative Protestant church. Jim says that his father was a harsh and driven man who was cold and even brutal towards his children. He states that he never saw his father touch his mother, and relates several instances of physical abuse that he suffered at his father's hand. He also characterizes his father as "uncommunicative," and notes that when his father did speak to him it was often to criticize:

JIM: I've thought of it a lot in terms of psychological
development too:......you know in the sense
that..............((strikes table?)) I think
abou:t.........I ha- had some deep
psychological:.....deprivations   (5)
and.....{whatever}.........#you know I had a fa:ther who
was totally # ....really uncommunicative.............a father
who:.........didn't know how to show- I never saw him touch
my mother.......you |kno::w|
INTERVIEWER: |MM|..........   (10)
JIM: u:h....he was actually ((dec)) physically abu:sive to
us at ti:mes............u:m.....a father
who:.............took me asi:de once when I
was:......perhaps:.......I don't know early high school I
THINK......TOOK ME ASIDE in the bar:nyard....and told   (15)
me....that...........he'd been watching me he said ((voice
change)) I been watchin you he says I got you figured
ou:t.........he said you're lazy you ain't gonna amount to
nothin............|(ha)|
INTERVIEWER: |hm| (20)
JIM: {isn't that a} NICE GIFT TO GIVE YOUR SON

Jim regards himself as having been reconciled with his father after the latter's death, in part through the intermediation of a psychic, a person who claims to be able to communicate with the spirits of the dead. The essence of this story is that a psychic told him that his father realized that he had treated Jim unfairly as a child and asked for his son's forgiveness. After this experience, Jim began to have dreams in which his father appeared as a benevolent and encouraging figure, and eventually a dream occurred in which Jim and his father embraced and were reconciled:[1]

JIM: the REVERSAL started happening. . . .in NUMEROUS dreams
over a period of about two years. . . . . . . .where the father
is. . . .giving, me and #it was getting to be that time in mid
life too where I was realizing that# I had this: LA:CK OF   (25)
THE MASCULINE. . . .you know ASSERTI ASSERTIVENESS that I
should have GOTTEN from the FA:THER. . . .|you know|
INTERVIEWER: |uh huh|
JIM: and I was feeling the need of that very deeply right
then. . . . . .so this went ON I had MANY MANY dreams   (30)
like tha:t and it sort of culminated in:. . . .(although) he
still enters dreams now as a kind of ARCHEtypal wi:se
man. . . .you |know|
INTERVIEWER: |uh huh|
JIM: in my dreams. . . . . .eh::. . . . . . .((voice change))   (35)
#this drea:m #. . . . . .it was provoked by uh. . . .an
instance where one of my co-workers. . . . . . .had a son who was
kill:ed in California:. . . . . .the father had
unfinished business with the son and. . . .you know he's a
friend of mine he invited me over just to be with him and   (40)
his wife . . . . .and um. . . . .((voice change, speaking
louder)) something about that provoked a dre:am in which I
was:. . . . .in a squa:re. . . .roo:m ((voice change, aside)) which
felt very Californian because of the. . . .(a) round ARCH on
each. . . . .{you kno:w side of the ro:om}. . . . . . .and I   (45)
was ((voice change)) I was looking out and there was a kind
of a harvest scene out there with SHOCKS of. . . . . . . .of gr-
corn you know. . . . . .and uh:. . . . .#all of a sudden
I saw out of the corner of my# ey:e I saw my father sitting
the:re looking very benevolent. . . . . .   (50)
INTERVIEWER: uh huh. . . .
JIM: and I #walked over to him and he pulled a# watch out of
his pocket. . . . . . .I'm not sure what that was all
about. . . . . .YOU HAVE TO GET INTO THE LANGuage of dreams you
kno:w the symbolism of dreams to talk about things like   (55)
this. . . . . . . .it seemed like he was saying you know either
you know. . . .time is running out or this is the ti:me #you
know |what I mean|
INTERVIEWER: |uh huh|

JIM: it had to do with time # 'h. . . . . . . .and then I just had   (60)
this overwhe:lming love for him you know and (the) tears
came- were in my eyes and were in his eyes #this is ALL in
the dream #
INTERVIEWER: yeah right
JIM: and we hugged one another in the most lo:ving   (65)
wo:nderful embra:ce. . . . . . . .and uh. . . .so:,. . . . . .((voice
change)) what really happened to me then is
tha:t. . . . . .in a kind of pos:t. . . .mortem you know
wa::y,. . . . .((voice is more expressive at this point))
I had this reconciliation with my fa:ther. . . . .and I now   (70)
love- I really love the man now
INTERVIEWER: uh huh =
JIM: =you know I felt like (I) made a lot of connection of
some kind. . . . . .AFTER ((voice almost chokes on word
"after")) he was dead you know. . . .all that- a lot of that   (75)
damage that he did was undo:ne. . . . .
INTERVIEWER: you |(s)|
JIM: |I don't|. . . .pretend to ex- {you know to know=}
INTERVIEWER: =to explain it

This passage reveals the essential characteristics of Jim's style. The first
point that should be noted is the variations in speaking style that occur
within these lines. The transcript notes "voice changes" of some sort at
lines 35, 41, 43, 46, 67 and 69. These changes occur as Jim moves in and
out of narrating his dream. Lines 35 and 41, for example, are points at
which Jim is beginning to tell the dream. The voice change at line 43
occurs when Jim temporarily exits the account in order to make a
comment on dream interpretation; at line 46 he returns again to the dream
in a special voice. (Although it is not marked as a voice change, lines 53–60
also constitute such an aside which is discussed immediately below.) Lines
67 and 69 contain changes as Jim leaves the dream account.

Although in fact the pattern is not particularly well-represented here, in
general Jim tends to tell his dreams, or parts of his dreams, in a voice that
is clearly distinguishable from the voice (Hymes 1979; Hill 1990b) in which
he converses with the interviewer. At times the voice of this dream
narrator is acoustically distinguishable, along dimensions such as tone
and loudness of voice, but the main indicators of the "dreamer's" voice
are not acoustic. In particular, Jim uses a rhythmic speaking style in
narrating dreams that is very similar to the effect of speaking in verse. This
style is evident in lines 42 through 53, where long pauses and word stress
repeated at regular intervals begin to set up this poetic style of speech. This
pattern is broken by the aside which begins in the middle of line 53. Here
the features of the dreamer's voice disappear as Jim comments on the
proper approach to dream interpretation, a fact which supports the

contention that he is using a special voice to narrate the dream. This new voice is very evident in the transcript, for this aside contains none of the rhythmic quality that marks the dream account, and the entire aside is set off by pauses at lines 53 and 60, the beginning and end of the aside.

The distinction between narrator's and dreamer's voices is one manifestation of a style of narration that pervades the interview. This style can also be observed, for example, by attending to the way Jim expresses emotions. In spite of his apparent willingness to discuss emotion-laden topics such as his anger at his father, his sense that he lacks masculine assertiveness, and his dreams, in fact Jim expresses little emotion during the interview. Careful attention to his speech reveals that he rarely discusses the current situation. For the most part, Jim reveals himself through memories of the past, episodes from his encounters with "paranormal" or therapeutic experiences, or (above all) dreams. His accounts of these phenomena, which are told as involving strong emotions, are themselves either unemotional or else marked by a sort of intellectual enthusiasm. Thus, for example, Jim often follows his accounts of dreams or other phenomena with the comment that they are interesting or fascinating.

This style of expression parallels Jim's style of dream presentation. In both contexts, Jim consistently separates himself as narrator from himself as experiencer. In the interview he is first of all not the dreamer, he is not acting emotionally; rather he is the fascinated observer of himself the dreamer or himself acting emotionally. From this perspective, the adoption of the dreamer's voice is a means to separate the person talking in the interview from the dreamer. In general, this aspect of Jim's narrative style has a paradoxical effect, for it allows him to build an effective wall between the speaker and the person being so intimately revealed in the speaker's narrative.

In the passage above, however, this separation breaks down for a moment as Jim describes his reconciliation with his father. This reconciliation has occurred (one must assume) entirely in Jim's imagination. Nevertheless, it is emotionally salient for him, as there are a number of signs in the transcription, beginning with line 69 and culminating in the "flooding out" (Goffman 1986) at line 74, which indicate strong emotion. Thus this set of events constitutes an exception to the generalization above, for here Jim does not separate himself from his emotions but rather integrates them into his narrative. This is not the only place in the interview where emotions are expressed in the wake of accounts of dreams or similar experiences involving fantasy; another example of this phenomenon will be discussed below. These episodes are in a sense the inversion of a stylistic technique such as the dreamer's voice, because in them the narrator and emotion come together; an emotional experience is not only recounted, it is re-enacted (Goffman 1986: 504).

Such exceptions to Jim's general style of self-presentation offer an opportunity to discuss in some detail what I mean by shifts in metaphoric and canonical communications. Throughout the narrative, Jim stresses that he is a psychologically sophisticated man who is at home talking about and expressing his emotions. That is, this message is conveyed referentially. At the same time, Jim works to create a particular situation, that of two intellectuals discussing religion, in which the focus of attention is on "interesting religious phenomena that have occurred in Jim's life." The activities Jim undertakes to create this situation are also communications, in this case of a constitutive type. These communications convey a rather different message than that Jim insists upon in his statements; on this level, Jim is uncomfortable with his emotions and loath to expose himself. But in the passage above, this situation begins to change.

Consider first the slip at line 62, where Jim corrects himself after initially starting to say (presumably) "the tears came to my eyes." This slip is another example of a constitutive communication, in this case a communication of a metaphoric type. That is to say, it is an initially opaque (non-referential) communicative behavior. The slip is also construable; it may be drawn into the realm of the referential. It is very probable that Jim decides not to use the phrase "tears came to my eyes" because in fact tears did not come to his eyes, he is describing a dream. Or, somewhat more accurately, Jim has two purposes that come into conflict here: he wants to preserve the impression that he is describing a dream, and to reveal his conviction that this was not a dream. For, after all, much here supports the conclusion that Jim regards the dream as something more than a dream. His attitudes about his father change as a result of how his father acts in the dream; that is, Jim evidently gives his actual father credit for the benevolent behavior of the image of his father in the dream. It is as if Jim regards the dream as a visitation from his father's spirit.

Thus I am suggesting that Jim has conflicting aims, he wants to give testimony to two opposing possibilities: it was a dream, it was not a dream. The situation is beginning to change. Instead of sustaining his distance from his narrative, Jim begins to become involved on a new level, to express his own ambivalence. Then, starting at about line 67, Jim summarizes the effects of the dream with uncharacteristic emotion, culminating in the momentary flooding out at line 74. Here Jim is no longer describing his feelings at a distance nor is he sustaining the appearance of his separation from the narrative. The feelings are present as Jim speaks, there is no separation between the situation and what is being described.

Jim is ambivalent, and in this passage the desires that for the most part remain hidden take over from his general level of control. Jim has, for a moment, become the emotional and expressive man he claims to be. What has allowed this inversion to take place?

What has happened here can be understood as a manifestation of the canonical, of the enduring, of that which is beyond this world. For Jim, as for many members of our society, a dream is a mystical phenomenon, something with a mysterious connection to everyday reality. And a dream of his father is a manifestation of an image of indisputable cultural and personal significance. The dream thus creates a context in which Jim can experience normally unacceptable aspects of his own feelings and desires, in this case about his father. That is, the sort of common sense that demands he be consistent and communicate coherently also offers him an opportunity to break out of that pattern in realms of discourse that are acknowledged to be beyond reason. As was the case with Jean, an aim (here, to express love for a father) that cannot be realized in the complicated context of social reality can be realized in a canonical context.

Of course, here the canonical has little if anything to do with Evangelical Christianity. In my experience, this is not unusual. Jean, for example, converted while trying to communicate with a tree, not an activity that many Christian theologians would endorse from a doctrinal viewpoint. Evidently, however, no one has questioned Jean about this in the intervening period of almost twenty years in a way that could shake her understanding of this as a Christian conversion. In general, the actual language used by the Evangelical Christians I spoke to is remarkably syncretic, drawing upon diverse sources such as popular psychology, popular understandings of Eastern religions, spiritualism, and so on. What makes this language canonical, in my treatment, is not its invariant formulae (although there are some of these) but its drawing upon the mystical, the infinite, upon that which has significance beyond the everyday.

Much remains to be clarified about the processes whereby the canonical and the metaphoric come into contact. Such contact occurs at several points in this interview, and will provide an opportunity for further study. I will argue that these processes are a technique whereby Jim has managed in part to transform his image of himself. First, however, I must say something more about that image.

Power and masculinity

I have shown that Jim's style of self-presentation in the interview involves a split between the narrator and the person who has the emotional experiences being narrated. I have also mentioned that this pattern breaks down at a few places in the interview. Setting aside the latter point for the moment, I now want to argue that Jim is aware of his own style – although he does not conceive it in precisely those terms – and that his involvement with the language of Evangelical Christianity has grown out of an attempt to change that style. My intent here is to explain, in general terms, the basis of Jim's interest in a canonical language such as Evangelical Christianity.

To do so brings me once again to the issue of intention. Many aspects of style may be modified through effort; one may work on one's writing style or dancing style. Style in the sense that I am using it here, however – style of self-presentation – seems to be for the most part outside the realm of conscious intention. This follows almost necessarily from the nature of style of self-presentation. If my style of self-presentation is my overall approach to doing things, then any attempt to change that style will itself be carried out in that style. Jim's situation provides a good example. At some point in the past, it seems, Jim decided that he was not sufficiently open, that he did not express his emotions in the way he would like to. His attempts to transcend this problem are in part what lie behind the somewhat paradoxical situation that can be observed in the interview. It is evidently Jim's conscious intention to express emotions, for he talks at length about many emotional issues. However this intention is itself carried out within the framework of a rather closed and non-expressive style, the result being that Jim presents himself as having emotional experience, but as being separated from that experience.

Simply intending to change one's style of self-presentation is not likely to be effective. Rather, my thesis here is that modification of personal style – a change in identity – depends upon being able to change certain constitutive communicative behaviors that are not produced intentionally. Such change may come about through metaphoric behaviors being drawn into the realm of the referential, so that previously non-intentional behaviors enter the realm of articulation. This may happen to the believer who devotes his searching attention to the relationship between a canonical language and his experience.

Jim, for example, has spent a great deal of time and effort in an attempt to fathom his own style. Jim's understanding of his own style is primarily expressed through rhetorical figures involving power and its relation to gender. Thus, for example, at lines 25–27 above, Jim says that he lacks masculine assertiveness and that this quality should have come from his father. This is one manifestation of a pervasive theme, Jim's complaints that he lacks power, energy, assertiveness, and so on. These complaints reflect an actual situation, for as has been shown, it is indeed the case that Jim is a man who is very often separated from his own emotional power.[2]

Because this situation troubles him, Jim has been drawn to discursive systems such as gender ideology or pop psychology, systems which offer various explanations of his difficulty. The conventionalized referential meanings of the symbols making up these systems give him a means to label and explain his "lack of power." By far the most basic and pervasive of the rhetorical figures Jim uses in the interview come from American gender ideology, which holds that men are more vigorous, more assertive, and stronger than women, and therefore identifies masculinity with power. Thus, in terms of the conventional meanings of the ideology, Jim's lack of power becomes a lack of masculinity. A causal relationship is asserted: as a male, Jim should have power. Although he never says so outright, many of Jim's comments seem to hint that the reason he lacks power is that powerful women close to him have prevented him from seizing the power that should be his. Of the many examples that could be called upon here, one of the most interesting is Jim's description of his wife, a woman whom he initially described as being "overwhelming like my mother." When I asked him to clarify just how this woman had resembled his mother, Jim responded:

JIM: (ha) well she was an exceptional #woman I'd met her in   (80)
Ne:w Yor::k, #....when I was in school....she'd come to New
Yor:k to: study:....music she was........very, #I was taken
to # her: intelligence and....her very ebullient
ver:y..........uh emotionally sensitive....bri:ght.....{you
know} lady............{overwhelming like my mother}   (85)
INTERVIEWER: oh REALLY I that's I was gonna ask
JIM: {yeah}
INTERVIEWER: | cause ((indistinguishable))|
JIM: |I realized| later you know that I just
really.......just-.......drawn to an overwhelming wom- you   (90)
know (a) VERY POWERFUL woman just indeed as my mother had
been, truthfully....|(HA)|
INTERVIEWER: |okay ((indistinguishable))|
JIM: |indistinguishable|
INTERVIEWER: like your mother in her::......in her: power   (95)
JIM: in her power right I rec- .... like- J:une was just what
Jung calls an anima personality I mean she's so
powerful....
INTERVIEWER: uh huh
JIM: #she was the kind of woman if she was in the middle of   (100)
a room (indistinguishable)#......you know she would- uh she
would get the ener:gy vortex ((dec)) going |around|
INTERVIEWER: |uh huh|

JIM: her: you know what I |mean|
INTERVIEWER: |uh-huh| uh-huh. . . .   (105)
JIM: a:nd it was really <u>characteristic</u> of our marriage that
I would be <u>out here</u> on the edge somewhere and she'd be over
there in the center. . . . #you know what I mean# with all the
energy. . . . . .around her
INTERVIEWER: energy d-do you mean people? (ha)   (110)
JIM: yeah
INTERVIEWER: {uh huh}
JIM: the interpersonal: |(dynamics)|
INTERVIEWER: |uh huh|
JIM: ((indistinguishable))   (115)
INTERVIEWER: all: ri:ght

The theme of power and masculinity manifests itself not only in Jim's
discussions of his wife and his mother, but also in his description of the
series of dreams which enabled him, after a long period of estrangement
from Christianity, to return to the faith in which he had been raised. This
series of dreams, which occurred over a period of several years, illustrates
very well the possibility of shifts between metaphoric and canonical
communications.

Through the process of dreaming and attending to his dreams, Jim
gradually adapts symbols from a number of different discursive systems to
the specifics of his own situation. The symbols that make up Jim's dreams,
like those that make up his thought in general, have conventionalized
referential meanings. For example, as has been noted, masculinity is a
symbol for assertiveness and power. This referential meaning is established socially; it is a part of the system I have called gender ideology in
American culture. However, the symbols that occur in an actual dream are
also constitutive in function, for such symbols constitute the situation of
the dreamer. After all, we experience dreams as if they were really
happening.

Thus the dream may be a locus of interchange between constitutive and
referential functions of symbolism. Symbols that have manifested themselves through a not consciously intentional process, the dream, may be
linked to the referential meanings contained in cultural systems such as
Evangelical Christianity. As such, the dream may be used as a means of
"discovering" personally significant versions of canonical symbolism. The
end result is that the symbols are no longer merely conventional, nor are
they completely idiosyncratic; rather they are meaningful on a personal
level. This process is best explicated through an example. The following is
an account of one of the earliest dreams in the series that led to Jim's
rediscovery of his faith:

JIM: but then <u>soo:n a:fter tha:t</u> comes:. . . . . . .began some
drea:ms <u>about</u> the <u>year:ning</u> to cut <u>loose</u>, ((dec)). . . . . . . .to
get <u>free</u> of a lot of this heavy-. . . . . .for EXAMPLE I dreamed
a very <u>vivid</u> dream I was driving <u>horses</u>,. . . .a team of   (120)
<u>horses</u>. . . .
INTERVIEWER: uh huh. . . . . .
JIM: u:m. . . . . .just <u>driving</u> them and ((voice change)) #I
don't think it wa- there was anything behind the #
<u>horses</u>. . . . . . .((voice change)) and <u>suddenly</u> the <u>horses</u> began   (125)
to <u>run</u> away:,. . . . . .and they're going FASTER and FASTER and
the reins. . . . . . .e- el- el- ELONG:GATE. . . .AS THE HORSES RU:N,
RIGHT? ((smile voice))
INTERVIEWER: uh huh |uh huh,|
JIM: |SO THE| HORSES ARE RUNNING AWA:Y. . . . . .and u:h as   (130)
they <u>run awa:y?</u> and they get abou:t fifty or sixty <u>yards</u>
they suddenly become ai:rborne. . . . . .you know like
the <u>myth</u> of. . . .P:egasus you know,
INTERVIEWER: uh huh |uh huh|
JIM: |among| the Greeks the <u>horses</u> are <u>airborne</u> and they're   (135)
WA::Y up in the <u>air</u> like a <u>kite</u>. . . . . .and I'm
WATCHING in ama:zement and boy thes (ha) THE REI:NS? RIGHT,
INTERVIEWER: uh huh
JIM: and uh. . . . . .suddenly,. . . . .I see <u>off</u> to the left a
hurri-. . . . . . . .a tornado <u>spou:t</u>. . . .coming =   (140)
INTERVIEWER: =uh huh
JIM: <u>ga:thering</u> momentum,. . . . . . . .so I <u>grab</u> my son
Sa:m. . . . . .RUN into the house, ((voice change)) drop
the reins, RUN into the house, RUN into the basement. . . .and
WAIT the coming stor:m you know   (145)

It is interesting to compare this dream account to Jim's description of
his wife. Both passages are concerned with images of great power, in one
the wife, in the second the tornado. Indeed, the wife is not so different
from a tornado in that she is referred to as the center of an "energy
vortex" at line 102. Furthermore, both of these power sources have the
same effect on Jim, namely that they chase him away. In the description of
his wife, Jim is chased away from the social center, the admiration of
others. In the description of the dream, Jim is chased away from his flying
horses. The final situation is in both cases the same: Jim is separated from
power, as he is in his very style of self-presentation.[3]

These horses are interesting in their own right, for one could argue that
they have sexual, specifically phallic, connotations. The action of the
horses in the dream account, at first proceeding as horses will do along the
ground and then rising up as the reins "elongate", would in many
interpretations qualify them as a grandiose phallic symbol. The problem
with such an interpretation, in the absence of other evidence, is that the

interpretation of any dream is difficult without considerable information about the dreamer. Furthermore, because of the setting in which this dream account was recorded, the connection of account to dream is particularly problematic. It has been years since Jim had the dream, he has worked it into a story he tells himself and others about himself and his life; all these facts suggest that the account may be a less than accurate description of the original.[4]

However, by attending to style, the immediate evidence of how the dream is related, one can go beyond the interpretation of dream symbols as such. There are two points where stylistic aspects of Jim's speech suggest that the horses are a phallic image. The first is when Jim chooses the word "elongate" to describe the extension of the reins; this word is of course infrequently encountered, and when one does encounter it it is very often being used to describe an erecting penis. And then Jim clearly betrays his concern that he should not use this word, I would guess because on some level he realizes he is revealing too much by using it. Thus this generally fluent man needs four tries to finally produce the word. These slips are clear evidence of ambivalent aims: Jim both wishes to reveal the sexual content of this dream and to conceal it.

The second piece of evidence of phallic imagery is not available in the transcript, although it would be in a videotape. At line 137, where Jim is describing the action of the reins, he was sitting in his chair, holding his hands above his lap about a foot apart, and shaking his hands rapidly to indicate the power and tension of the reins he was holding. The gesture, in other words, depicted something of throbbing power pointing upwards from Jim's lap.

Thus when Jim is forced to drop the reins by the advance of the tornado, he is abandoning a symbol of tremendous potency. The similarity of Jim's wife to the tornado, noted above, suggests that the tornado is a symbol of feminine power. This interpretation is again compatible with a straightforward symbolic interpretation of a psychoanalytic type, since the tornado is a clear (if grandiose) symbol of the female genitalia. (I am referring to the fact that the tornado is dark and triangular in its two-dimensional depictions, while up the middle of the tornado runs a "funnel," a channel like the vagina.)

This dream account demonstrates how Jim's understanding of his own situation, a reconceptualization of a "lack of power" as a "lack of masculinity," has pervaded his mental processes. The dream seemed significant to Jim precisely because in it his own understandings of himself become part of his actual experience; in the terms I have introduced here, the symbols involved function constitutively in the dream. Jim subsequently examines these symbols, and finds that they can be interpreted as referential symbols from discursive systems such as gender ideology or Evangelical Christianity. The effect is to enhance his level of commitment to these systems, which seem to be perfectly adapted to his situation.

Shifting from the canonical to the metaphoric

This sort of process is not the only form that shifts between constitutive and referential forms of communication take in the process of commitment. As noted earlier, in Evangelical Christianity it is above all the shift from canonical language to a metaphoric function that seems to be associated with the increasing commitment that accompanies the conversion experience. Consider, as an illustration, the following dream, the full version of the dream with which I began this book. This dream represented something of a turning point in Jim's life, for it gave him a sense of power and of religious awakening:

JIM: SO::
INTERVIEWER: uh huh
JIM: the on- biggest one of the biggest drea:ms I guess that
I had on the spiritual quest then ca:me ((dec))....in
seventy si:x...............like a foretaste of things to   (150)
come ((speech noticeably slow)).........this brings a lot of
tha:t together......it's #I bet # the single most powerful
drea:m I've had from the high self....you might
say...........I drea:med that I was um....in a
city.......((voice change)) the Olympics were going on in   (155)
Montreal at that time......((voice change)) I was in a
city.....at the top of a
hi:ll.....................an::d.....I was sitting up in a
tree:?, ((very precise diction, as if one were telling a
story to a child)).......a great big tree:,..........an:d   (160)
it was morning....and I had this sense of:...........a new
day beginning....{you know....a new
day}.........an:d........a ritual was going on I- there
were buildings arou:nd ((voice change)) not
unli:ke..........buildings (that) we have here at the   (165)
university......I remember two buildings in
particular..............it was daw::ning.............an:d
ah: out into the balcony....of a second floo:r, came an
o::ld man and a young man....again right? ((smile
voice))......and this time they're.....they're they   (170)
hang:.......out on the balcony: (a-) a banner and a
fla:g.........((voice change)) I don't recall which one had
the banner....you know, and which one had the fla:g.....but
there was a kind of pageantry to announce a new
day....starting |right?| (175)

INTERVIEWER: |uh huh|. . . . .
JIM: and I wa:tched that. . . . . . .with this feeling, you kno:w
of kind of exci:tement and. . . . . .forward
looking. . . .feeling. . . .and then SUDDENLY as sometimes HAPPENS
in dreams out of the corner of my eye again. . . . I saw this   (180)
frie:z:e. . . . . .a frieze, you know, that's
a::. . . . . .sto:ne |you know {with a}|
INTERVIEWER: |OH YEAH| okay, yeah
JIM: with a sort of three dimensional=
INTERVIEWER: =yeah=   (185)
JIM: cut. . . .about. . . .twenty to thirty feet hi:gh ((whisper
voice for emphasis)). . . . . .and on this
frie:ze there was a pictur:e that was a picture of a
combination of CHRIST on the CROSS and a Greek
a:thlete. . . . . .VERY powerful. . . . # you know what I   (190)
mean? # this wonderful combination of. . . . . . . .of the Greek
and the Christian. . . . .and POWER # you know I mean I just #
s:. . . .like it's CHRIST on the CROSS but it's not this
ema::sculated ((dec)). . . . .
INTERVIEWER: uh huh   (195)
JIM: this ema:sculating:. . . . . .sort of thing. . . .I'm-
I'm. . . . # putting my own interpretation # into the dream
now,. . . . . . .and I looked at that,. . . .and it was very
interesting becaus:e. . . . . . .it was very POWERFUL and
there were still in the nooks and crannies of   (200)
this:. . . . . . .of this:. . . . . .frieze. . . . . . .there was STRA::W,
this was something FRESHly unPACKED. . . . . . .and there were
bits of STRA:W and bits of tinfoil YOU KNOW LIKE IT HADN'T
FULLY COME FORWARD YET that there was still some
INTERVIEWER: {uh huh}   (205)
JIM: JUNK AROUND that I,=
INTERVIEWER: =uh huh=
JIM: =you know. . . . . .but it was VE:RY POWERful the
symbol, and then I: ((voice change)) couldn't stay in the
tree any longer, the tree was kind of hollowed ou:t. . . . .and   (210)
open, and one- I have a tree in my. . . .yard li:ke
that. . . . . . .and I found myself coming RIGHT OUT of the
tree:,. . . . . . .and with the feeling, ah, now I have work to
do. . . . .
INTERVIEWER: {{uh huh}}. . . . .   (215)
JIM: {I- I have} to express:. . . .this (on some plane)
INTERVIEWER: uh huh. . . . . .
JIM: BUT, {you know I look back on that dream} and it seems
like the- # one of the most powerful drea:ms #

As noted earlier, Jim generally narrates his dreams in a voice that is
different from the voice he uses in the interview as a whole. This dream
provides perhaps the best example of the dreamer's voice. As Jim prepares

to narrate the dream, his speech slows, at line 149, and this slow speech continues throughout the first half of the dream account. At line 154, with the words "I dreamed that", Jim begins to narrate his dream. Almost immediately he interrupts his own account with an aside at line 155; as was mentioned above, the fact that the aside is spoken in a voice acoustically distinguishable from the voice of dream narration highlights the fact that two separate voices are involved.

As Jim returns to his account of the dream, the dreamer's voice is once again immediately evident, both because of its clear diction and its rhythmic, repetitive quality. This section of the dream account could easily be broken into verse on the basis of the pauses and stress that the dreamer introduces into the narration:

> I was in a city
> at the top of a hill
> and I was up in a tree
> a great big tree

This rhythmic pattern continues, interrupted by another aside in the voice of the narrator, until the vicinity of line 172, where the pattern breaks down. Here Jim re-enters a pattern which is typical of his narrative style in general, fluent but marked by numerous tag questions such as "right?" and "you know?" These tag questions are probably intended to bring the interviewer into the narrative (Briggs 1986: 109), and the interviewer is indeed much more involved in the account up to line 183, where he grasps the idea of the frieze.

Note that at line 180 Jim uses the phrase "out of the corner of my eye again," creating a parallel to line 139 above, where he says that he spotted the tornado "off to the left."[5] This is not the only link between these images. In the former dream, the image of power appears in two parts. The first form of the image, the flying horses, has masculine connotations and is specifically linked to Greek mythology at lines 132–135. The second form of the image, also appearing in the sky, is the tornado, an image of power with feminine connotations. In the latter dream, there is one image of power, but it is presented as a "combination," something that is composed of two parts. Those two parts are a Greek athlete and Christ. Like the horses, the athlete is linked to Greek culture; Jim's description ("not emasculated") also may indicate that the image is specifically masculine, that is, that it has a visible penis. (Greek athletes, of course, often competed nude and are often depicted in that state.) The other part of the image in the latter dream is Jesus Christ. Recall here that since the nineteenth century, Jesus is apt to be depicted in much of American popular religion as heavily feminized (Douglas 1977). Portraits of the deity depict Jesus as having soft features, long hair and flowing robes; so-called feminine psychological traits such as gentleness and passivity may also be attributed to him. Thus, like the images of power in the former dream, the horses and the tornado, the image in the latter dream seems to have specifically masculine and feminine halves. All told, there is a noticeable continuity between the images of power in these two dreams.

The second part of the dream is narrated in a style that is not typical of the dreamer's voice, for it lacks the most important characteristics of this voice: slowed speech, dramatic pauses, verse-like prosody, and absence of tag questions. The stylistic features of this part of the account are indicative above all of excitement. At line 187, the second half of the dream is introduced with a dramatic whisper. In this section of the dream account, Jim invites more participation from the interviewer and mixes elements of the dream with comments on its proper interpretation, as at lines 193–198. Although such asides also occur in the first section of the dream account, there they are noticeably set off from the account, whereas here they are integrated into it.

Jim's excitement is clearest at lines 204–209, where the volume of his voice increases noticeably as he discusses the symbol he has conceived. These lines form the culmination of the account, the revelation of the power of the symbol, a "combination of the Greek and the Christian," a masculine Jesus.

Jim says that this dream had certain important consequences in his life. In the first place, he says that this is the "single most powerful dream" he has ever had and indicates that it was a very important dream in his "spiritual quest." Although Jim does not assign his conversion to a particular moment, he considers this dream to have played a significant role in his return to faith. And finally, Jim suggests that this dream was an important phase of his discovery of his own "power."

Jim's excitement as he tells of the central image of the dream, the combination of a Greek athlete and Jesus Christ, makes it clear that the importance of the dream is due in large part to this one image. Why should a particular image have such significance for Jim? From a perspective that considers only the referential meaning of symbols, it must be assumed that once Jim located the proper image, a meaning could be conveyed that made a remarkable difference to him. The fact that the image was a version of something that had evidently been occurring in his dreams for some time would seem to support this assumption. Previously, images of power had been split between a satisfying but inaccessible male component and an overwhelming and threatening female component. In this dream Jim was finally able to synthesize the two parts to come up with an accessible – because masculine – image of power.

In spite of the undoubted relevance of these observations, I doubt very much that they are sufficient to explain the role of this image in Jim's commitment to Evangelical Christianity. If the significance of the symbol were somehow contained within it, then it would follow that at any point someone could have simply suggested this image to Jim and he would have felt all the powerful effects he attributes to this dream. Anyone with even a passing familiarity with psychological change will recognize this as an implausible assertion. It is not intellectual knowledge that can change a person's situation, it is knowledge in context; significance stems as much from how the person accepts the liberating knowledge as from what that knowledge is. This is not to say that the referential meanings conveyed by this particular image are not important. But those meanings are not sufficient in themselves to explain the significance of this image to Jim. In order to understand what the image of the masculine Jesus does for Jim, then, one must look not only to what the image is, but also to how it is used (Crocker 1977: 45).

In general, as has been shown, Jim takes pains to separate himself as the present narrator from his powerful dreams. Dreams are sources of power to Jim, and dream accounts reflect this by being narrated in a style that is split off from his overall narrative style; the voice of the dream account is measured, poetic, perhaps even oracular. In this separation, Jim's emotional situation is depicted with the utmost clarity: he is indeed a man who lacks power, in the end because he separates himself from his own power. Time and again in the interview, Jim portrays himself as having emotional or powerful experiences, but in most cases, these experiences occur not in everyday life but in realms of the imagination. This pattern also manifests itself in his narrative style, in that for the most part Jim is careful to separate himself from the figure experiencing these powerful events.

This pattern breaks down, however, at several points: in the latter part of the narration of this dream, in the description of his reconciliation with his father, and at a few other places in the interview. In these moments, the ability of dream or fantasy to enter into present experience is affirmed, and Jim is himself infused with the emotional power the dream presumably contains. Jim's style of self-presentation, the very "powerlessness" that so concerns him, is transformed at such junctures. In that these experiences are also associated with certain canonical symbols, for example in the most recent case with the symbol of the powerful Jesus/athlete, these canonical symbols transcend their purely referential function, coming instead to function constitutively.

That is, in the narration of this dream, the meaning of the canonical symbol of the powerful Jesus/athlete is not purely a matter of meaning as reference. Rather, the image has merged with Jim's experience. As Jim tells of the powerful image of a Jesus/athlete he conceived in a dream, that image enters into his very style of presentation and empowers the narrator. But this moment cannot be explained as resulting from the efficacy of a particular symbol or from a simple change of style by the actor. Rather, a symbol and particular style occur together to create an experience that is felt but not necessarily known. In this experience, the efficacy of the canonical image is demonstrated to the believer in a new way, for that image does not label or merely parallel but rather constitutes his or her experience. The believer comes to *experience* the image and his commitment to the system of which it is a part grows.

In this way the canonical image comes to serve as a mediator between a canonical language and lived experience, and thus comes to function both referentially and constitutively. Silverstein (1976: 24) has written, in regard to referential indexes, that they

anchor, as it were, the semantico-referential or quasi-semantic mode of signs, those which represent pure propositional capabilities of language, in the actual speech event of reference, by making the propositional reference dependent on the suitable indexing of the speech situation.

To put it in different language, referential indexes mediate between the referential function of language – its ability to encode propositions – and its ability to correspond to an actual, ongoing situation. The referential index is the point where the realm of the referential hooks up to the social world in which lanuage is spoken. Constitutive communicative behavior, which I introduced by comparing it to the referential index in language, works in a similar way on the level of canonical language. That is, by coming to function constitutively, a canonical image links a language such as that of Evangelical Christianity to the specifics of a particular life and situation.

In the case under consideration, a canonical image (once again syncretic) of Jesus as a Greek athlete comes, through Jim's narration, to constitute a particular possibility in his experience. This possibility is the realization of his for-the-most-part thwarted urges for potency and emotionality. The canonical image thus comes to function metaphorically in the special sense of that term, as an opaque formulation incorporating an aim that cannot be fully realized in most social contexts. It is in fact the very opacity of the image that accounts for its power: Jim feels, without fully interpreting, the potential significance of the image. It is the barrier to interpretation, the opacity of this image, that enables it to function as a receptacle for divine power, for the image contains a mysterious but palpable power. This is what I mean when I speak of shifting between the canonical and the metaphoric.

Throughout this chapter, I have attempted to demonstrate how self-transformation and commitment are generated in shifts between canonical and metaphoric communicative behaviors. It may be useful to review and summarize the claims I have made about Jim and his use of canonical language, particularly the language of Evangelical Christianity.

Jim's self-presentation as he tells the story of his increasing commitment to his religion is paradoxical. On the one hand, he is willing to discuss intimate matters such as his dreams and his sense that he lacks masculinity. On the other hand, he reveals these features for the most part through fantasy experiences and further distances himself from himself by attributing many of his feelings, dreams, and so on to a voice that is clearly separable from the narrator's voice.

The dominant theme of Jim's story is his conviction that he lacks masculinity and its associated power, having been deprived of these things first by his inability to identify with his insensitive father and subsequently by the important women in his life. Stylistic analysis shows that this description of his situation in the language of gender ideology is in fact valid, for indeed he does consistently separate himself from his own emotional power.

As Jim labels his experience with the conventionalized terms of discursive systems such as gender ideology and Evangelical Christianity, not consciously intentional aspects of his behavior such as dreams and style of speech begin to reflect the influence of these symbols. The stage is thereby set for experiences in which Jim discovers that some aspect of his own behavior produced by purposes he does not acknowledge is reflected in canonical symbolism. Such an experience, to take a single example, occurs when Jim finds significance in the fact that the Christian deity may be understood as a human male. He thereby finds that previously inarticulable aspects of his concerns about masculinity may be expressed with the help of Christian symbolism. What has happened, then, is that a previously metaphoric communication (the appearance of Jesus Christ in a dream) has begun to be appreciated in referential terms, as Jim is able to name Jesus' masculinity as significant for him. Such experiences, in which the believer recognizes the referential functions of symbols previously experienced as constitutive, strikes him or her as insight. The believer sees a higher significance, a meaning in that which had been present, but not acknowledged, in his or her behavior. The underlying transformation here is, in my terms, the articulation of previously embodied purposes.

The "other side" of this process occurs when an image that has previously been understood in referential terms comes to constitute ongoing experience, and in so doing attains a new level of significance. In the case discussed here, such a movement can be observed in those moments when Jim temporarily suspends a central characteristic of his own style, his separation of himself in the present from himself having emotional experience. When this happens, a canonical image enters Jim's experience and allows him to fulfill an aim that is for the most part thwarted in social experience. The canonical thereby comes to function as a metaphor in that it becomes a constitutive communication formulating an embodied aim. And in this way the believer's commitment to the canonical language may be considerably deepened, for he comes to appreciate the power of parts of that language in his own life.

5   Miracles

I have suggested that the opportunity to formulate embodied purposes in a canonical language may lead not only to a stronger commitment to the canonical language but also to a transformed identity. A change in identity occurs because the believer experiences relief from pressure to perform actions that he regards as ego-alien (because they mesh poorly with self-conception); such relief seems to coincide with the formulation of aims in canonical rather than metaphoric terms. Here I would like to look more closely at this process of change whereby, through a shift from metaphoric to canonical communications, the believer is able to abandon behaviors that he previously felt *compelled* to undertake.

To be compelled is, most broadly, to consistently express purposes through action and language that one wishes to deny having intended to produce. One produces without consciously intending the compelled thought or action. In one sense, compulsion may be contrasted to control. Controlled behavior is behavior that corresponds precisely with one's conscious intentions. In spite of the seeming contrast, however, control and compulsion often appear together in the action of a single person; by this I mean that a person who conveys the impression of being highly controlled may also be subject to compulsions. It may well happen that a person who has experienced compulsions tries to circumvent them by increasing her level of conscious control over her behavior. Similarly, the attempt to carefully control one's behavior may issue in compulsions, the expression of purposes one does not recognize as one's own.

Several persons I interviewed during the project were notable first of all for the extraordinary amount of control they attempted to exert over the interviewing process. In at least two cases, this guardedness was so consistent as to render attempts at analysis very difficult. These people agreed to speak to me, but in doing so seemed reluctant to reveal much about their religious convictions or themselves. On the other hand, in other cases noticeable attempts to control the interviews were not in themselves an insurmountable obstacle to analysis. Here the very attempt to control the direction of the interview itself manifested patterns that were revealing.

These latter subjects are of particular relevance for this inquiry because I assume that those who seek to control the interview process are persons who are quite concerned with control in other areas of their lives as well. In fact, I would argue that it is no mistake that both of the individuals described in this chapter had conversion experiences of the type that is perhaps prototypical of the Christian conversion. These conversions are, as one informant put it, "road to Damascus" experiences. That is, they are like the Biblical description of the conversion of Saul of Tarsus:[1] the believer is knocked off the path of his or her current life by a profound emotional experience that reorients the believer towards God.

The sudden conversion, which strikes the believer as ego-alien, as caused from beyond, is most likely to occur in a subject with significant unacknowledged purposes. That is, I assume the sudden conversion is an experience in which denied wishes and emotions manifest themselves in spite of the conscious intentions of the subject. Such profound inner conflicts are especially likely to occur among persons who do not recognize their own ambivalences. Thus I suspect that problems of intention are particularly likely to be illuminated by these interviews.

Larry, a retired executive

Larry is a retired executive now in his early seventies. He was born in Europe and emigrated to the US with his family when he was very young. He grew up in the Midwest near an urban center; his family were members in a conservative church, most of whose members came from ethnic backgrounds similar to Larry's own. In talking about his childhood, Larry stresses the strictness of his upbringing:

INTERVIEWER: ((five lines of text omitted))
|(indistinguishable)|
LARRY: |I GUESS| I guess you know WHA:T HA:PPENS
((microphone noise, he is touching the microphone with his
hands)) is that uh:.........I was BORN and uh and RAISED in
the ((ethnic reference deleted)) home.... (5)
INTERVIEWER: uh huh.......
LARRY: that should SAY a lot of things
INTERVIEWER: uh huh |sure (ha)|
LARRY: |right off the bat,|........uh:....I was born,....I
mea- I was raised in a very................uh:......strict (10)
INTERVIEWER: uh huh.......
LARRY: uh.........................uh wh- my:- my WHOLE

LIFE was, was was surROUNDed with strictness,. . . .you know
INTERVIEWER: uh huh
LARRY: you- ya can't you- you <u>don't</u> do this, you <u>don't</u> do   (15)
that
INTERVIEWER: sure |I know the old ((identifying reference
deleted))|
LARRY: |you don't do this|. . . . . .the only thing I will
say about it is that I:. . . . . .you: kno:w,. . . . . . . .I think
my mother and father were just. . . .marvelous ((microphone   (20)
noise continuing))
INTERVIEWER: uh huh
LARRY: uh:. . . . . .I'M,. . . .I'M TICKLED TO DEATH that
they:. . . .put the <u>clamps</u> to me. . . .on a <u>lot</u> of things

Larry shows many signs of agitation here, particularly in discussing the strictness of his upbringing. He picks up the microphone and begins to play with it, and his stutters and hesitations nearly disrupt his account. It may be that the interviewer's repeated interruptions and overlaps stem from a felt need to reassure Larry, to calm him down.

This level of agitation is not typical of the interview as a whole. Especially in the first half of our conversation, much of our time was spent on Larry's accounts of problems he had solved during his career in business. The interview began with a few questions about Larry's background, but I was unable to begin my normal routine of questions about childhood because Larry quickly launched into a discussion of his work experience that continued, with only minor interventions on my part, for about sixteen pages of typewritten transcript, corresponding to over eighteen minutes of speaking time.

From the beginning of the interview, then, Larry sought to present himself as a very competent professional who has been in high demand throughout his career because of his valuable skills. Not surprisingly, eventually Larry explained himself; he said he talked about his accomplishments not to boast but to explain that God has given him many gifts with which to serve others. Whatever the reason for Larry's discussion of his employment may be, this discussion certainly comprises an attempt to control the conversation he was having with me.

This style of self-presentation, of course, conveys something different than what is explicitly intended. Rather than developing the impression that Larry was a competent professional, I developed the impression that Larry was defensive, for reasons I probably could not know. He seemed overly eager to convince me of his competence, and so I concluded that he lacked confidence in his competence. And of course, Larry's somewhat crude techniques of impression management left me with a conviction that for some reason he had, at least in this situation, very little toleration for the ambiguities and flexibility that close interaction with another person demands.

This brings me back to the passage above and the topic of Larry's agitation. There is a tendency in Larry's self-presentation to undermine points that he initially seems to insist upon. For example, he insists that he has no hard feelings about his strict upbringing, but he has a great deal of trouble simply saying this. Furthermore, he presents himself as a highly competent, hard-headed business man, but then – to my mild surprise – begins rather abruptly to narrate a "healing experience" he had had while he was a young man. From a defensive and controlling posture, Larry shifts to a seemingly open and vulnerable one: he had been suffering from a long illness, had lost a good deal of weight, and evidently had not responded to medical attention. The paradox of this admission of vulnerability in the context of discourse so energetically constructed to deny any vulnerability is reflected in Larry's method of introducing this topic.

LARRY: uh: in about nineteen ((microphone noise, handling
microphone)). . . . . .about nineteen   (25)
thirty-ei:ght,. . . . .
I had a. . . . . .I had
ah:. . . . a ner:vous. . . .breakdown,. . . . .
INTERVIEWER: {mmm}. . . . .
LARRY: if you wanna call (i)t that, ((speech slurred)) wha-   (30)
what it rea::lly was,. . . . . . . .that caused the,. . . . .the
breakdown,. . . . . .uh:I? had
developed. . . . . . . .uh,. . . . . .uhw:a, A:Bscesses, #in my
tee:th, #. . . . .
INTERVIEWER: {uh},   (35)
LARRY: a:nd? uh,. . . . . .and SO the
ABSCESS. . . . . .ha:d uh,. . . . . .the
poison. . . . .had got(ten) me right (i)n the- in the: uh,
INTERVIEWER: uh huh
LARRY: in: the: ((strikes table)) uh. . . . . .central part of   (40)
the nerve systems,. . . . .
INTERVIEWER: uh huh
LARRY: a:nd #so that #. . . . . .just really,. . . . . .knocked a hole
in me. . . .
INTERVIEWER: |uh huh| (45)
LARRY: |well?|. . . . . .u:m. . . . . .I was
in? summer school at the time. . . . .((sniff)). . . . . .but I:
had ta,. . . .I fi:nally had ta dro:p outta: that, particular
summer school,. . . . .#I had?- I# DROPPED one
subject, so that I: wouldn't ha:ve a ((dec)) full load,   (50)
INTERVIEWER: uh huh. . . . .
LARRY: an: THEN UH:. . . . . .I didn't DROP SUMMER schoo:l,
{altogether} I just dropped the one,. . . . .well: I think I

dropped <u>three</u> units (a)nd..........carried just three ta
finish <u>out</u> I think it was   (55)

Larry begins by relating that he suffered a nervous breakdown around
1938; the fact that this admission is difficult for him is evidenced by the
two very long pauses preceding this statement. He then immediately
goes on to retract the claim he suffered a nervous breakdown, insisting
instead that whatever symptoms occurred were a result of abcesses in his
teeth. The second version is much more in line with Larry's self-
presentation, for in American society a nervous breakdown is often
seen as a shameful indication of some deficit in one's character. Thus it
makes sense that Larry, who stresses his competence and confidence,
would prefer a biological over an emotional/mental explanation for his
illness.

But if this is so, why does Larry begin by attributing his illness to a
nervous breakdown? This question is merely a more specific version of the
one above: Why even discuss this set of events if the goal is to present
himself as competent and always in control? The problem is compounded
as Larry continues to speak, for at lines 48–49 he states that he dropped
out of school, and then once again immediately retracts and modifies this
account. It was evidently only one course that he dropped. In this case, as
in the previous one, Larry states something that emphasizes that he was
having trouble, then retracts the statement, replacing it with a statement
that to some extent denies he faced a serious problem.

All of these observations point to ambivalent aims: Larry's intention to
control the interview is countered by a desire to reveal facts about himself
that contradict the image of one always in control. And that impulse in
turn is modified by subsequent denial of his own loss of control. As Larry
continues to relate the story of his healing experience, the pattern expands.
It turns out that the experience occurred in the midst of a prayer service
that Larry was attending with his father (he stresses that his mother was
away at the time):

LARRY:...............a:nd my #Dad n I'd# gone to the <u>prayer</u>
service, that was a Wednesday
night,...............((sniff))....and we'd gone to the
PRAYER SERVICE
there...................................a:nd....Pastor
Davis was,...........................was   (60)
um,..........leading the <u>service</u>?...................a:nd,
I think he was <u>right</u> in the <u>midst</u>, as <u>I recall</u>, he (wa)s
#<u>right in the midst</u># of uh:,.............ah
uh........giving: exposition on so:me #part of the scripture,#....

INTERVIEWER: uh huh. . . . .   (65)
LARRY: ((very mysterious tone of voice here)) ((dec)) a:nd
all of a sudden. I
can't?. . . . . . .I KNOW it,. . . .I KNOW it's the Lord,. . . . . .I KNOW?
THAT,. . . . .(ha). . . . . .uh:. . . . .
. . . . .told me;,. . . . . .uh:. . . . . .see THAT'S WHY,   (70)
you know #sometimes hard {t:} talk about these, # cause
people- #it's hard for people t: understand
these. . . .things. . . . . . .
INTERVIEWER: sure. . . . .I know, (ha). . . . . . .
LARRY: uh::. . . . . . . .a:nd the lord? said to   (75)
me:,. . . .Larry. . . . . .you?. . . .what you have to
do:. . . .RIGHT NOW. . . . . .is that you have to have
((voice change, urgent)) NOW THIS ISN'T BY VOICE. . . .I MEAN
THIS IS. . . . . .uh you uh you have it's. . . .((microphone
noise)) it's something you can't explain,   (80)
INTERVIEWER: uh huh
LARRY: anyway that. . . .you can't 'h
. . . . .but. . . .THAT. . . .you HAVE TO HAVE. . . .your da:d,
your fa:ther?. . . . . .DISRUPT the SERVICE. . . . .
INTERVIEWER: your father disrupt |the service| (85)
LARRY: |my:| yeah =
INTERVIEWER: =mm hm
LARRY: AND TELL:. . . . . .PASTOR. . . . . .uh
Davis. . . .tha:t. . . . . .that um. . . . . .that I
need prayer   (90)

During the service, Larry is seized by an impulse – which he takes to be
the word of God – to have his father disrupt the service. Here it is not
Larry's need for prayer that is foremost, with the disruption of the service
an unfortunate secondary effect. Rather, the demand for disruption is
presented as primary, with Larry's need for prayer as the reason for the
disruption.[2] This need for disruption parallels Larry's behavior in the
interview, in that it reflects the presence of a motive to disrupt that which
is controlled. Thus, first of all, one can observe here the same pattern that
has characterized earlier interviews: the subject's behavior in the interview
manifests the same ambivalence that is depicted in the story the subject
tells.

This still leaves the fundamental problem, however. Why should
Larry's behavior manifest such clearly conflicting motives? What does
the presence of a strong motive to disrupt indicate in the context of
a self-presentation for the most part oriented towards control? Larry
seems to have two aims, both very strong, that are directly opposed to
one another. Together, they create the impression of a compulsion,

a demand to control and an equally strong rebellion against that demand.

It is significant to note that in the narrated experience, it is none other than God himself who gives voice to the motive to disrupt. I have argued that the motive to disrupt is most accurately conceived as an unacknowledged aim of Larry's. Thus, once again the canonical language is serving here as a medium through which unacknowledged purposes may be expressed. In attributing the motive to disrupt the service to God, Larry's unacknowledged aim is transformed. In the context of the prayer service, a spontaneous contribution from God is no disruption at all but rather a miraculous confirmation of the efficacy of the event: God is thereby shown to be present and responsive to the ritual. Thus, the effect of the disruption is not to put Larry's faith into question but rather to confirm the strength of that faith:

LARRY: and so <u>we</u> LEFT THE.......we LEFT the:
uh:........meeting and <u>someone else took
over</u>?........................((voice change)) and it
didn't- #but for some reason or the other the spirit didn't
allow# disrupt ((slurred speech)) didnterrupt (a thing)   (95)
it-....just-......he just <u>left</u>?..........and <u>came</u> with
us..............
INTERVIEWER: oka:y....
LARRY: a:nd-....and <u>we:</u>? went upstairs....and- an you
don't-.....we're DOWN IN THE BASEMENT now,....so the FIRST   (100)
FLOOR is the AUDITORIUM........|sanctuary|
INTERVIEWER: |okay|
LARRY: then the SECOND FLOO:R.....would be the
BALCONY.......
INTERVIEWER: all right..............   (105)
LARRY: SO: <u>we went up</u> ((aspiration on p becomes
sigh))......................to: {the}- to: uh....we went up
to the: <u>first floor</u>..........((Larry is playing with
microphone)) and the DOORS were LOCKED,......|to|
INTERVIEWER: |uh huh| (110)
LARRY: the..............to the: uh <u>main auditorium</u> or (wh-)
and um........................so:........Pastor Davis
said well: why don't we just kneel <u>right
here</u>........................((click with tongue)) and
uh........<u>so:</u> we knelt down there? ((click with   (115)
tongue))................................and THIS GOES RIGHT
ALO:NG WITH JAMES NOW, IF YOU'VE EVER READ THE S-FIFTH
CHAPTER A JAMES WELL YOU'LL KNOW WHAT I'M TALKIN ABOUT
INTERVIEWER: okay.................
LARRY: uh:.................Pastor Davis.....<u>put</u> his <u>hand</u> on   (120)
my head

INTERVIEWER: uh huh. . . . .
LARRY: and <u>started</u> to <u>pray</u> for me. . . .and I? told?
him. . . . . .that it <u>had to be</u> you know that
I:. . . . . .<u>knew</u> that <u>Christ</u>. . . . .((voice softer)) would   (125)
<u>heal</u> me. . . . .
INTERVIEWER: huh. . . . .
LARRY: that's. . . .hɔw my <u>faith</u>. . . .was I really- and I <u>knew</u>
it. . . . . .I (w)as <u>positive</u>. . . .
INTERVIEWER: uh huh. . . . . .   (130)
LARRY: and I'M STILL POSITIVE. . . .#{if there's something
wrong with you}# he would <u>do that</u> if ther- if |THAT WAS|
INTERVIEWER: |uh huh|
LARRY: his WILL now
INTERVIEWER: uh huh sure. . . . .   (135)
LARRY: a:nd when <u>he</u> put <u>his hand</u> hand on <u>my head</u>. . . .and
started #praying for me#. . . . . .it was LIKE if
you ha:d a:. . . . . .FIVE POUND BOOK ((strikes table))
lying right here
INTERVIEWER: uh huh   (140)
LARRY: on this desk
INTERVIEWER: uh huh. . . . .
LARRY: whew. . . . .<u>that's</u> how I felt. . . .((slightly slurred
speech)) (that leaving me)
INTERVIEWER: uh huh   (145)
LARRY: just like that. . . . .
INTERVIEWER: huh. . . . .
LARRY: and from THAT MOMENT O:N. I
DIDN'T. . . . .#WHICH (IN) MOST CASES YOU DON- I DIDN'T
GET WELL# ((snaps fingers loudly)) just like THAT. . . .   (150)
INTERVIEWER: uh huh. . . . .
LARRY: 'H but. . . .THAT- FROM THAT MOMENT ON is when I started
getting <u>well</u> right away

Larry begins by noting that the effect of the "disruption" was in fact not
that disruptive, and then goes on to describe in some detail the floorplan
of the building in which his healing experience occurred. This is a common
rhetorical technique for establishing the accuracy of a narrative: detail
about place is invoked to support the unspoken contention, "I'm not
making this up, this is a real place that I can describe in detail." As is often
the case in Larry's narrative, he exhibits here a concern with establishing
the veracity and certainty of his story.

The healing ritual conducted by the three men is said to parallel the fifth
chapter of James, another miracle, that of the re-emergence of Scripture in
contemporary experience.[3] Larry is adamant at lines 125–129 that he knew
that the ritual would result in healing. This conviction echoes that
expressed in a previous passage at lines 68–69 where Larry insists that he

knew that the order to disrupt came from God. Again, the theme of conviction and certainty (as in Larry's insistence that he appreciated his parents' strictness) turns up.

Thus this passage can be said to heighten the tension that characterizes the interview as a whole, that between Larry's asserted conviction and certainty and the consistent underminings of that conviction. The narrative expresses both sides of Larry's ambivalence, just as the healing experience did. To summarize: the conversion narrative is a ritual form; in this it is similar to the church service in which Larry's healing occurred. Furthermore, the ritual of the narrative becomes the occasion for the eruption of Larry's unacknowledged aims to disrupt the ritual order; again, this is precisely what happened in the healing experience. But in both cases, narrative and healing experience, the end result is not disruption but confirmation of faith, for the ritual is able to embrace the disruption. Larry feels the presence of a force he believes to be from beyond himself; but in the ritual context the ego-alien quality of that force convinces him that it has a transcendent source.

In the healing experience Larry utilized a technique that he still uses in the narration of his story, disrupting that which is ordered as a means of demonstrating his faith. Disruptions create a window in which the efficacy of God may be demonstrated. If Larry were indeed able to perfectly control his life and his narrative, there would be no need for God. But he has found a way to express his ambivalence about control within a framework that makes that ambivalence a sign of his faith, an opportunity for a miracle.

Alice: control and that which is beyond control

This theme, the possibility of relinquishing personal control in order to, from the perspective of the believer, let God take over, also manifested itself in what was probably the most difficult interview I conducted in this project. My subject was a retirement-aged woman whom I will call Alice. My discomfort during the interview arose because of the sensitivity of some of the material that Alice brought up and the nature of the interaction that occurred in connection with this material. Alice had a son (Howard) who committed suicide, and she struggles to make sense of this painful event. She feels that her incessant prayers on behalf of her son, during his lifetime, were never answered, and has evidently concluded that his death was simply a part of God's inscrutable plan, something that was for the best in a way she cannot understand.

Alice speaks a great deal of miracles, and she believes that a miracle occurred in her life shortly after her son's death. An acquaintance of another of her children (Barry, Alice's oldest son), who lived abroad, received a letter from Barry telling her about the suicide. Upon reading the letter the friend experienced certain strong feelings, even though she did not know Howard personally:

ALICE: BUT.............when she read in Barry's
letter,.........i:t just well::ed over her:.........a   (155)
feeling............tha:t....................uh one of
God's O::WN had gone HO::ME and everybody there was happy
and rejoicing....'h and that this:.......child, ((voice
change, breaking)) {now twenty-nine....years old,}
was.........h:appy ((voice change, very expressive)) for   (160)
the first time in his life....'H and she: rejoiced.....BUT
SHE DIDN'T KNOW WHY? ((smacking sound)) she couldn't
understand any of this..............cause {{uh}} suicide is
something that..........anybody is uh:......it's repugnant,
it's it's ama:zing, it's......'h SCA:NDALOUS, it's uh: (165)
'h.......H:O:RRIBLE, it's,........................and, I
me- it's just something that nobody can possibly cope with,
and especially if you don't know the situation you know,

This passage is notable first of all for a Biblical tone of speech, especially at line 161, "and she rejoiced." Using terms that recall the Bible in order to depict this event, Alice is of course exploiting a rhetorical device to support her claim that this is a miracle. Another thing that is conveyed in this passage is Alice's basic moral attitude about suicide; it is, to say the least, unacceptable to her.

Alice knows of the friend's reaction because of the fact that, shortly after having received the letter, the friend happened to be passing through the town where Alice lives as she traveled home. She called Alice, whom she had never met, and asked to meet Alice and her husband at the local airport. Alice begins by explaining that as they traveled out to meet the friend at the airport, she worried about what they would talk about:

INTERVIEWER: |uh huh|
ALICE: |and I was| going to find out all these interesting?   (170)
things? I mean that's what you talk to somebody about |that|
INTERVIEWER: |yeah|
ALICE: comes from.....'h....that part of the wo:rld and a
((identifying reference deleted)) and all uh, you know,....
'h (#was gon-#) WE:LL.....she wasn't interested in THA::T,   (175)
she wanted to know about Howard, 'h.....and she:.....told
me th th this, but sh first......'h she wan(ted) to know
((speech slurred, sniffing)).........w:hy he was in
trouble.....'h she went clear back....to the pre-natal
situation 'h......u::h...........ALL the things that went   (180)
in to tha:t......and his comin up life.....and #this that

and the other thing # that she was. . . .consu:med with
that. . . . .'h a:nd. . . .we talked for h:ours and h:ours almost
three of well ALMOST (FO-) THE FOUR HOURS, =
INTERVIEWER: =uh huh=   (185)
ALICE: = about Howard. . . . . . .a:nd. . . . . .from then on. . . . .God's
message to me ((dec)) was that things were-. . . . .were all
right. . . .and that he was safe. . . . .|and|
INTERVIEWER: |uh huh|. . . . .
ALICE: he was where I would. . . . .   (190)
INTERVIEWER: uh huh
ALICE: #see him again someday #
INTERVIEWER: uh huh. . . . .
ALICE: and that was good
INTERVIEWER: uh huh   (195)
ALICE: 'h and I haven't. . . . . .uh REA:LLY. . . .you
know shed #very many # tears since then because
'h. . . . . .he is happy
INTERVIEWER: uh huh. . . . . . . .uh huh
ALICE: and what more could I want for him. . . .|you know| (200)
INTERVIEWER: |uh huh|
ALICE: so that's great
INTERVIEWER: uh huh that sounds {yeah} pretty miraculous
((slight laugh here))

At the beginning of this excerpt, one may observe in Alice's stated
concerns a characteristic of her interactional style. Faced with the
prospect of meeting someone new, Alice is concerned about how the time
will be spent, and attempts to plan the encounter. The friend, however, is
consumed with the desire to talk about Howard. It is possible (since the
friend was a religious functionary) that Alice regards this person as a
direct representative of God, since she takes the friend's assurances as a
message from God.

For my purposes, however, the most salient aspect of this excerpt is the
final line, where I react to the story Alice has told. This final response is, of
course, a lapse in empathy. Although the laugh is sympathetic, a more
astonished reaction was being solicited. As might be expected, I was not
consciously aware of this lapse at the time I made it, but looking back at
the transcript my lack of empathy is obvious. There is no need to comment
in detail on my own feelings here, other than to say that I was not in
complete sympathy with Alice's way of coming to terms with her son's
suicide, and I was evidently unable to disguise this fact from her.
Predictably, the relationship between Alice and myself deteriorated
rapidly from this point. First Alice begins to implicitly question my own
religious perspective, implying that she had talked to me only on the
assumption that I shared her Evangelical views:

ALICE: {{(oh well)}}....and (it's) just, 'h
there......there
every day:........there are 'h there are little mir-   (205)
miracles that.......that you <u>share</u> with <u>friends</u> and....
INTERVIEWER: uh huh
ALICE: and <u>they</u> with <u>you</u>
INTERVIEWER: {uh huh}
ALICE: {{so}}....   (210)
INTERVIEWER: {I see how that works}....I think so ((soft
laugh)) (indistinguishable)
ALICE: um.................you- you..............h-
it's....a thing that you <u>h:ardly</u>.........<u>talk</u>
about.............((sniff)) t- to somebody............that   (215)
doesn't sha:re wh- <u>where</u> it comes from,
INTERVIEWER: UH HUH
ALICE: you know 'h........uh- I mean you wouldn't try
explaining a miracle to somebody who....is not a believer

Alice turns next to a discussion of how she felt betrayed when another
interviewer on religious topics turned out not to be sympathetic to her
religious views:

ALICE: I: I ma:de the mis<u>take</u> ((clicking sound)).......of   (220)
talking to um..........a, g o:h a woman that lived be<u>hind</u>
me...............((clicking sound)) one time,
((sniff))....................in ((location name
deleted))............she was a, a parapeligic.....
INTERVIEWER: um   (225)
ALICE: <u>quadrapelegic</u> really....and uh:......was studying
psychiatry....
INTERVIEWER: uh huh
ALICE: and she was <u>married</u>.......a:nd u:h....became
interested in <u>religion</u>........((smack or tapped something))   (230)
(per se)........'h s:o she w- became interested in
me:........a:nd......became interested in.....ALL things
#(in the church)# I took her to Billy <u>Gra:ham</u> I took her to
<u>church here</u>
INTERVIEWER: uh huh   (235)
ALICE: she became <u>interested</u> in <u>Seekers</u> [an adult Sunday
school group to which Alice belongs] 'h.......a:nd
u:h.....she: <u>wanted</u> us ta.....to <u>do</u> some <u>work</u> on her <u>paper</u>
'h.....and uh ((clicking
sound))...................................I was SHOCKED   (240)
when I read her {th}....her dissertation
INTERVIEWER: uh huh
ALICE: ((clicking sound)) and: it hurt a:ll, I haven't
told <u>anybody</u>....except you
INTERVIEWER: uh huh uh huh.......   (245)

ALICE: and uh:. . . . . .h:ow, a- about her
dissertation ((smack)). . . . . .a:nd it was a:ll? ve:ry
ve:ry tongue in cheek,. . . . .'h what kind of people are
converted. . . . .
INTERVIEWER: hm. . . . .   (250)
ALICE: ((smack)) and uh are they rich are they poor are
they. . . . . .educated are they uneducated. . . . .
INTERVIEWER: um
ALICE: uh: all of this. . . .business
INTERVIEWER: uh huh   (255)
ALICE: a:nd really a ve:ry very. . . .tongue in cheek attitude
about the whole? thing and we had
spent,. . . . . .a uh like two? years. . . .with her

Alice continues to discuss this situation, and then notes that her efforts
to influence the researcher's religious views had been ineffective:

ALICE: doesn't matter. . . .(ha) you know
'h. . . . . .so. . . . . . . .but I- we were I think we were (260)
a:ll kind of hoping that. . . . . .through our effort and
our testimony that it would make some effect (in) her life
INTERVIEWER: uh huh uh huh |sure|
ALICE: |but I| don't think it ever did. . . .I don't
think. . . . .| well if it did| (265)
INTERVIEWER: |well you never know though|
ALICE: no. . . . .
INTERVIEWER: you never know. . . .because I th- I know you
kno:w I've been doing this kind of work =
ALICE: =yeah=   (270)
INTERVIEWER: =and I've certainly been very affected because
ALICE: yeah
INTERVIEWER: {uh}
ALICE: BUT. . . .I think you were a Christian (ve) fir:st
before. . . . . .uh by   (275)
INTERVIEWER: uh huh
ALICE: the people that you know:
INTERVIEWER: uh huh
ALICE: I I know. . . .{that you are. . . .you see} so that makes a
difference   (280)
INTERVIEWER: uh huh we:ll,
ALICE: otherwise I wouldn't have been willing to |talk to
you at all|
INTERVIEWER: |ha|

Here, the issue that was raised at lines 218–219 becomes explicit, and
Alice comes close to directly asking about my beliefs. My reactions allow
Alice to conclude that I share her religious views, in spite of the fact that I
was consciously avoiding saying this to her directly. (My reasons for doing

this have to do not with my role as a researcher but rather with my beliefs as a person. I do not share Alice's religious views.)[4]

I have quoted extensively from these sections of the interview in order to illustrate the relationship that developed between Alice and me during the interview. These exchanges made me acutely uncomfortable. Alice's hostility toward the earlier researcher, evident at line 226, where she emphasizes the researcher's handicap, is an implicit threat. She is convey-ing the message that I must not be like the earlier researcher. Furthermore, Alice insists at lines 218–219 and 274–283 that I hold certain religious beliefs, otherwise she would not have told me the things she has. But, of course, she has told me these things. This puts me in the position that causes my discomfort, a sort of "double bind" (Bateson, Jackson, Haley and Weakland 1956): Alice tells me what my goals as a researcher and my religious beliefs must be. Not only does Alice attempt to control her relationship with the interviewer, but as she becomes angry she does so in a way that tries to define the interviewer's beliefs. I take Alice's interaction with me as strong evidence of what she is like outside the interview; she is a person who attempts to exert considerable control over the behavior of others.

This contention can be supported by other sorts of material from the interview. Alice speaks much of the plans she made for the members of her family, but also recognizes that her tendency to do this can get out of hand. In fact, Alice's conversion, as well as most of her religious experience in general, seems to be oriented around an attempt to mitigate her attempts to control events. The story of her conversion itself provides a good example of this.

Alice's conversion

Alice's conversion occurred when she was a married woman in her early thirties. In describing the conversion, Alice mentions first that she had been attending a church where the liberal minister did not believe in certain miraculous elements of the Christian faith such as the resurrection and the virgin birth:

INTERVIEWER: um- they do. . . .now do you think that they were   (285)
#glossing it over in the church# or you felt that you
didn't. . . .you didn't really believe |those things (that
you-)|
ALICE: |the church| itSE:LF was glossing over it. I
DIDN'T realize what I wasn't hearing. . . .   (290)
INTERVIEWER: uh huh =
ALICE: =because we had a really a wonderful speaker there in

the church there. . . .in ((place name
deleted)). . . . . .a:nd
um. . . . .((exhaling, a sigh, then a   (295)
clicking sound)) he was the #kind of person# that-
. . . .that. . . . . .was a lot of fun and we all liked to
be with,
INTERVIEWER: uh huh
ALICE: a:nd uh. . . . .((clicking sound)) I   (300)
just really wasn't? hearing? what? he? either was saying or
wasn't saying,. . . . . . .until one da:y. . . . . . .Ea:ster. . . . . . .he
came right out and said that. . . .he didn't. . . . .that there
#was ah no such thing as the r- resurrection# ((mumbling
voice))

This passage is interesting because of Alice's use of the negative. At lines
289–290, she says, "I didn't realize what I wasn't hearing." The last four
words convert the negative to a positive, in a sense, in that what the
preacher wasn't saying becomes the focus of the sentence. This sort of
formulation is repeated nearly every time Alice mentions this experience.
For example, at lines 301–302, she states that she "wasn't hearing. . . .what
he wasn't saying." And in a later passage that I have not reproduced here,
she says, "I was ready to hear the nothingness that that man was
preaching," a formulation that again singles out a nothingness as a
something, something very important.

This aspect of the rhetoric of Alice's conversion story works to link her
previous religious life to her experience in general before the conversion.
Alice hints at significant difficulties in her life in the period before her
conversion, but never directly comes out and says what was bothering her.
One formulation that occurs early in her story is as follows. (The referent
of "it" in line 310 is the experience just described, the encounter with the
liberal minister):

ALICE: and I thi:nk ((dec)). . . .I was searching   (305)
mySELF. . . . . .for a closeness that I didn't
ha:ve. . . . .
INTERVIEWER: {uh huh} ((someone is speaking in the
background))
ALICE: a:nd. . . .for something that I was really missing in my
own life. . . . . .and tha:t's. . . . . .WHY: it kinda   (310)
pulled the rug out from under me

Here Alice says she was looking for a closeness she didn't have and that
there was something missing. It is of course not significant in itself that
Alice uses the negative in discussing problems in her life, for this is a
common practice. However, these formulations occur repeatedly and
consistently in her speech. In the following passage I summarize Alice's

position and she confirms my understanding with a series of overlapping
affirmations that seem to indicate close agreement:

INTERVIEWER: uh huh yes I:
ALICE: {uh huh}
INTERVIEWER: (act-) I do......that's....something I
hear....a <u>lot</u> about |that| (315)
ALICE: |uh huh|
INTERVIEWER: in a sense <u>before</u> you....convert
that........you've got to realize that there's something
<u>missing</u> |in some|
ALICE: |uh huh| (320)
INTERVIEWER: way and that you.........
ALICE: uh huh?
INTERVIEWER: #that you need something and so# that
you.......you had <u>felt</u> that maybe your <u>faith</u> was sort of
thin....and you said you- you felt the need for closeness   (325)
was it closeness to <u>Go:d</u> or |personal|
ALICE: |YES|
INTERVIEWER: closeness
ALICE: a <u>personal</u>......there,
yes....UH:......................((clicking sound)) w-   (330)
where ALL of us....where I
was......<u>praying</u>..............i::......in for- a- uh-
because of desperate <u>nee:d</u>....I was praying..........but to
an absolutely empty heaven,
INTERVIEWER: {uh huh}.....   (335)
ALICE: u:m..and
m- my prayers were not being answered..............
INTERVIEWER: uh huh
ALICE: a:nd......you just go on #praying, praying praying
praying praying# a:nd nothing is <u>hap?pening</u>, nothing is   (340)
<u>changing</u>....in fact thi- things seem to be gettin # worse
worse worse,#

Once again, at line 334, a strong negative formulation occurs, "an
absolutely empty heaven." The question becomes, what is missing? What
lack do all these negatives designate? From Alice's testimony, the answer
to this question must be sought in her relationships to her husband and
her father, for she goes on here to discuss this topic. She refers first to her
husband's having been away in World War II, saying that the separation
had been difficult for both of them:

ALICE: and uh..............<u>due</u> to the....
probably due to the <u>wa:r?</u>......my- and Frank
was overseas   (345)
INTERVIEWER: oh I didn't |know that|

ALICE: |a:nd| yeah. . . .and du:e to u:h. . . . .((clicking
sound)) maybe a lo:ng engagement and by the time you get
married. . . .a lot of the romance is go:ne
INTERVIEWER: sure   (350)
ALICE: and you're just real good frie:nds,
INTERVIEWER: uh huh
ALICE: and then you even lose that a little
bit. . . . . .uh wh- wh- when ther- there's a lo:ng
separ- separation,   (355)
INTERVIEWER: uh huh
ALICE: uh due to the wa:r # and one thing and another and
uh # . . . .ma:il is rotten and. . . . .|you know|
INTERVIEWER: |uh huh| right. . . . . . .
ALICE: 'h a:nd. . . . . .so- my whole world my father is dead by   (360)
now, ((sniff))
INTERVIEWER: uh huh
ALICE: a:nd uh. . . . . .my h- my world is
just. . . .crumbled. . . .| # everything # |
INTERVIEWER: |uh huh|. . . . . .   (365)
ALICE: # everything # that was. . . . . .that-. . . . . .that- (ma-)
that gave me:. . . . . .a footing. . . .
INTERVIEWER: sure
ALICE: WAS GONE
INTERVIEWER: sure, |I understand that| (370)
ALICE: |my father was gone|. . . .and my husband. . . .wa:s gone
and then even when he's ba:ck he's really go:ne

Earlier in the interview, Alice had stressed the closeness of her relationship with her father and the fact that she admired him tremendously. She
says, for example, "I think I always had a very personal feeling toward
God, because he had to be like my father, you see." She recalls fondly a
period shortly before her marriage where her mother had to leave home to
be with Alice's sister, who was ill:

ALICE: I had ta stay H:OME and take care of my FATHER? cause
my mother had to be in ((place name deleted)) to be with my
sister. . . . . .so. . . . # by taking care of my fa:ther that   (375)
meant I # I was learning how to cook. . . .
INTERVIEWER: was |was|
ALICE: |um hm|
INTERVIEWER: he: was he
ALICE: 'h ((clicking sound))   (380)
INTERVIEWER: ill at the time?
ALICE: not my fa:ther no:
INTERVIEWER: oh
ALICE: |ah|
INTERVIEWER: |just you meant just| (385)
ALICE: |just RUNNING the HOU::SE|

INTERVIEWER: |you had to cook for him|
ALICE: |yes|
INTERVIEWER: |yeah okay| uh huh
ALICE: uh cooking for im an =   (390)
INTERVIEWER: = uh huh
ALICE: yeah?. . . . . .doing the things that. . . . . . . .you
know ironing his clo:thes and stuff |like that|
INTERVIEWER: |uh huh uh huh|
ALICE: gettin him off in the morning (ha)   (395)

This interchange contains an extraordinary amount of overlap, in this case indicating that Alice and I were having some trouble negotiating what to do. The problem begins when I am confused by Alice's statement that because her mother was gone, she had to take care of her father. This indicates, in the first place, a generational difference between Alice and me; I had trouble for a moment understanding why a grown man would need his daughter to take care of him. Of course, Alice simply takes it for granted that a man needs to be taken care of in terms of having his daily needs met, needs such as meals, laundry, and ironing. The overlaps occur as she tries to clarify and I try to reassure her that I understand, implicitly that I find it reasonable that a man would have to be taken care of.

There may be another explanation for the evident delicacy of this passage. I may have reacted to Alice's language – especially given the fact that this passage is embedded within her discussion of her early years with her husband – as indicating a relationship between Alice and her father that made me uncomfortable. Alice had spoken at length early in the interview about her admiration and love for her father, and here her story seems to indicate that she got a good deal of pleasure out of playing a housewife role while living with her father. I follow Freud (1964) in the assumption that many or all children must deal with the fantasy of marriage to the parent of the opposite sex, and one possible interpretation of Alice's speech and behavior is that she retained such fantasies into her adulthood.

Thus when Alice says that something was missing in her life, she is – as she says at line 371 – referring at the most basic level to her husband and father. Her father is gone and her husband is figuratively gone. It seems likely that Alice was feeling lonely, empty, and that a certain kind of closeness was missing from her life, for she uses these words in describing her situation. Her reference, at line 349, to the fact that much of the romance was gone from her marriage may mean that she felt she no longer loved her husband as she should, or it may mean that there were sexual problems in the relationship. Either of these would explain what she means when she says her husband was gone.

The language in which Alice describes the conversion itself supports these conclusions and enables further insight into the nature of Alice's problem around the time of her conversion. She starts by explaining that a neighbor, who could see that Alice was unhappy, invited Alice to go and see an Evangelist:

ALICE: so: very?. . . . . .wi::sely. . . .o:ne ni::ght
((voice change, storytelling voice)) she just # it was the
holy spirit I'm quite sure # no- no::w. . . . .
INTERVIEWER: uh huh
ALICE: that. . . . .pro:mpted her to say. . . . .'h (wo)- there's a   (400)
WONDERFUL speaker over at first pres and I mean university
pres
INTERVIEWER: uh huh
ALICE: ((smacking sound)) let's go?
INTERVIEWER: {uh huh}   (405)
ALICE: a:nd I nee:ded. . . . . . .that # so badly # and so I
went?. . . . .((smacking sound)) # with her, # ((name
deleted)) I don't know if you:'ve ever heard of hi:m or
not. . . . .
INTERVIEWER: {mmm}   (410)
ALICE: UH. . . . . .w- was # the minister # and
I don't remember to this day what it was. . . .
INTERVIEWER: {{uh huh}}
ALICE: that he: uh. . . . .ta:lked
about. . . . . .BUT. . . . . . .I n:-. . . .BUT   (415)
UP until then it was, # it was just getting building up to a
climax ((voice begins breaking here)) where my need for Go:d
was GREA:TER #. . . . . .was GREATER E:VEN, ((gains
control of voice here)). . . .than my need for Frank?. . . .
INTERVIEWER: uh huh   (420)
ALICE: it was GREA:TER. . . . .even than my need for my little
chi:ld?. . . .|who was|
INTERVIEWER: |uh huh|. . . . .
ALICE: two years o:ld by this (or-) time
INTERVIEWER: hmm   (425)
ALICE: or three. . . . .((smacking sound))
it was a- it was a consu:ming thing?. . . . .((sniffing
sound, she is crying)) my need f-. . . . . .n:eed for
Go:d. . . . . .a:nd uh. . . . . .SOMEWHERE? during the sermon,
I don't know, #. . . .I probably. . . .NOTHING that ((name   (430)
deleted, the preacher)) ever um: m-. . . . . . . .MEANT to sa:y
INTERVIEWER: uh huh?
ALICE: and I've talked to him talked to him about it
la:ter. . . . .and h-. . . . . .we just agreed? # that it was
the holy spirit that just convicted me and all of a sudden I   (435)
got burning hot #. . . . . .f:laming HOT?. . . . . . . .ALL OVER

AND I THOUGHT I WAS GONNA PA:SS OUT ((sniffing
sound))..........AND SO:............#I said to my friend I
have to get ou:t?# ((spoken without support, breathy))
((sniffing sound)).......so she (shqui-) took me out to   (440)
the....VESTIBULE.......and finally I got my breath
back.....................((sniffing and smacking sounds))
a:nd uh.............we stayed there until I......I: could
at....at lea:st even wa:lk....
INTERVIEWER: uh huh.............   (445)
ALICE: and w- so we left the chu:rch......and we went home-
and I went home,........A:ND from THEN ON I
FELT........that GOD was #RIGHT with me# every single
minute,.......
INTERVIEWER: uh huh=   (450)
ALICE: 'h =A:ND ((sniff))............NO:THING? THAT I HAD
EVER PRAYED FOR,......EVER CAME ABOU:T,
((sniff)).....EXCE::PT....ALICE WAS
DIFFERENT,.............((dec)) CONSEQUENTLY.........the
marriage became......absolutely.....P:ERFECT   (455)

The experience that Alice interpreted as the conviction of the holy spirit
would probably be interpreted in a secular context as what is often called
an anxiety attack. All of the classic features of such experiences are present
here: shortness of breath, dizziness and a fear of passing out, a flushed
feeling, and a pressing need to escape the situation. Although the etiology
of such experiences of overwhelming anxiety is a subject of controversy,
many observers have suggested that they are associated with the incipient
awareness of denied impulses. Something that the subject is unwilling to
acknowledge comes close to consciousness and provokes extreme anxiety.

By offering this parallel to Alice's conversion, I do not mean to offer the
reductionistic understanding that Alice's conversion was "nothing other"
than an anxiety attack. The latter term has no more claim on ontological
certainty than does "conversion experience." Rather, Alice experienced a
physiological response that some would call an anxiety attack, others a
religious conversion. However the experience is labeled, it is undeniable
that something is causing a strong physiological response in Alice at the
time of the conversion.

The cause of this response can only be an object of speculation, but it
seems reasonable to me to assume that she nearly becomes aware of an
impulse that provokes strong anxiety. It is noteworthy that the language
Alice uses to describe the conversion at the beginning of this passage
draws its figurative power from the experience of sexual desire. At lines
416–417, she describes her need for God as "building up to a climax,"
saying that the need was greater than her need for her husband. Earlier

references allow one to understand that this "need" is a need for closeness of some sort, a closeness that is missing in the marriage and which, because it is lacking, has created a lack of romance. Alice's need for God is compared to her need for her husband as well as for her child. This need for closeness, in other words, is being described in part by analogy to sexual experience. Alice goes on to use the term "consuming" in describing her need for God, and this is of course another term that is often encountered in descriptions of sexual experience, as in "consuming passion."

Just as I do not want to reduce Alice's conversion to an attack of anxiety, I do not wish to insist that Alice is, in an unacknowledged way, longing for a sexual relationship with God. I simply observe that the language she uses can be understood to convey such longing. To take the interpretation a step further, it has been noted that Alice says that her model for what God must be like is her father. Furthermore, Alice may have retained a strong fantasy of being her father's wife into her adult years; at the very least we can say that his death was a considerable and disturbing loss for her. All of this points to a complex of desires that Alice would certainly be loath to acknowledge, and which may be partially expressed in the form of the conversion.

The narration of the conversion itself is marked by frequent passages of rhythmic speech. An example is the first few lines of the story, where stress repeated at regular intervals informs the listener that Alice is preparing to tell a story (as in "Once upo:n a ti:me"). In general, the rhythmic speech marks off the entire passage as being of special significance, a performance of something central to Alice's experience and self-conception.

The story also contains considerable signs of expressed emotion, as in the sounds of crying (sniffing), the breaking voice, the numerous long pauses, and the bursts of loud, emphatic speech. What does this expressed emotion communicate?

The overall effect of the passage is quite dramatic. Rather than saying she felt flushed, Alice tells me she was "flaming hot" in a loud voice. As she recounts the moment of her incapacity – she had to escape the church – her voice loses support, as if to emphasize her helplessness. She pauses for over two seconds after saying that she had to get her breath back (line 442), and the whole of the account of these events is narrated while evidently only tenuously controlling an outbreak of weeping. The entire performance skillfully emphasizes the significant emotions of the earlier experience and gives the impression of nearly getting out of hand: the emotion is almost too much for Alice to be able to continue.

The best characterization of this performance may be that it is a tightly controlled loss of control. By this I mean that, like a skilled actress, Alice relives the emotions of her conversion experience in order to render it effectively, and this level of skill is to some extent in contradiction to the assertion that the power of this experience is so great as to nearly compromise the narrator's ability to recount it. In this Alice is like Jim, who had decided to express his emotions, but did so in a style that remained remarkably unemotional. Alice's conversion taught her that there were phenomena beyond her control, and now she attempts to come to terms with these phenomena by controlling them.

Such an interpretation fits very well with a more general impression of Alice and her religious experience. As I stated at the outset of this analysis, Alice's religious experience seems centered around the issue of control. What Alice's conversion taught her, with its experience of strong ego-alien impulses to collapse, was that she must turn over certain aspects of her life to God. In her own words:

```
ALICE: a:nd.................((door slams)) consequently
they could just........u:m....................be PU-
be....PUT i- in-the place in my life where they? should?
be,...........u:h...........................it- its
kind- its kinda hard hard to explain...........except          (460)
tha:t.............((slow,deliberate)) I wasn't
concentrating on the things that.....I- I thought had been
necessary before.....to change.......'h I'm the kind of a
person........of the school teacher type....of when
something goes wro:ng....you correct it                         (465)
```

In a way, Alice has learned this lesson, and looks for miracles as signs of God's control. She speaks a great deal of how she has learned to turn over to God certain phenomena that she would like to control but cannot. By this she means that she prays about these things – and for the most part these are situations that concern her husband and family – and thereby attempts to give up her attempts to control them more directly.

The form of the conversion and of its narration, however, make it clear that this characterization is an oversimplification. The point is not so much that Alice has accepted the necessity of yielding control as that she has integrated a degree of ego-alien intention into her experience. The physiological response of the conversion experience was, after all, caused by Alice herself. And the narration of the conversion flirts with a breaking down of the ability to narrate, an overcoming by the sheer power of the experience itself, but such a breakdown or overpowering never actually happens. Alice's loss of control is skillfully handled within the framework of a controlling style. And of course, Alice's turning control over to God is still an attempt to realize her own goals, through supernatural rather than secular means.

It is my impression – admittedly a tentative one, based on my limited contact with this woman – that Alice is a woman with little toleration for her own ambivalence. Her discussions of her father and of her conversion suggest that she retained into adulthood a common childhood fantasy, that which Freud described in terms of the oedipus complex. The material in this book shows over and over that believers often attempt to realize in their relationships to God aims that are forbidden in mundane society. Alice is no exception to this; in the conversion event she begins to become aware of her sexual desire in her relationship with God and is flooded with anxiety as her unacknowledged aim comes dangerously near to articulation. Lest this seem a fantastic claim, it should be kept in mind that sexually tinged relationships with the divinity are anything but rare, comprising a stock piece in the repertoire of religious asceticism.

As with other believers, Alice's conversion provides a paradigm for a technique of emotional management that enables a working compromise between her intentions and embodied aims. Alice presumably gives up aims she regards as destructive and shameful, such as the desire to control everything, and formulates these aims in her relationship with God. But, of course, she has not really given up her aims. Rather, she has found a less destructive means of formulating them.

Embodied purposes and divinity

This conclusion highlights certain features of both cases examined here. The nature of the change Alice undergoes as a result of her religious experience is complex. She adjusts to a world she realizes she cannot completely control by accepting the role of a force far greater than herself in determining the events of her experience. This is a force that she may petition, but whose purpose remains beyond her understanding. But at the same time, Alice weaves that which is beyond her control into her own purposes. In a sense, Alice's religious beliefs allow her to acknowledge and struggle with her compulsion to control. Her own unacknowledged aims are named, and thereby partially controlled, a paradoxical way of managing her compulsion to control that fails precisely to the extent that it succeeds.

In Larry's healing experience, his impulse to disrupt the church service was manifested as the voice of God. As a command from God it became an opportunity for a miracle rather than a disruption. Thus Larry learned a way to express his rebelliousness, his motive to disrupt, within a framework that renders that disruption a sign of his submission. Although it is not possible to know for certain, it is worth speculating that it is precisely the ability to express his ambivalence that cured Larry of his physical symptoms. Those symptoms, painful and disruptive as they evidently were, may well have been the expression of the body of emotions and thoughts that Larry was unable to acknowledge. What happened on that night half a century ago was that Larry discovered a new way of expressing his doubts and his pain, a way of expressing himself that was possible within the tradition in which he had been raised. In sum, although Larry's unacknowledged motives are rebellious and Alice's controlling, the two are alike in seizing upon the possibility of using their relationships with God to express their embodied aims.

There is a performative technique that remains outside the analysis here, and for that reason this chapter must remain somewhat incomplete. The technique I refer to is prayer, a verbal performance that is central to the religious lives of both of these believers. Petitionary prayer could be looked at as a verbal performance of intentions that are acknowledged but not realizable. From the perspective of the believer, prayer is often an attempt to make some situation occur by speaking it; in the terms introduced earlier, it is an attempt to make canonical language constitutive in a particularly concrete fashion. For the believer who has personally experienced shifts between referential and constitutive functions, for example in the form of a conversion, the claim that it may occur again has a ring of truth. As an Evangelical tract that has sold millions of copies has it: "Words are the most powerful things in the universe today" (Capps 1976: 25). The author asks, "If Jesus came to you personally and said, from this day forward it will come to pass, that everything you say will happen exactly as you say it; would that change your vocabulary?" (Capps 1976: 3–4) The message is that indeed this will occur for those with faith.

Once again, however, one is confronted with an old anthropological problem, that of manifest and latent function (Merton 1968). Assuming that one does not accept that petitionary prayer in fact has this sort of efficacy, what useful purpose does it serve for the believers who continue to practice it? S. J. Tambiah's (1968) observations, in his now-classic article "The Magical Power of Words," suggest the direction in which an answer should be sought. Tambiah shows, in an analysis of Trobriand gardening magic, that the ritual is addressed to the bodies of the participants, who are urged thereby to restrain their hunger: "It is the belly that 'hears' and 'understands' the rite which is externally performed on an inanimate object" (Tambiah 1968: 202). A similar conclusion can be drawn from this analysis. Verbal techniques of a ritual nature (including prayer) effect communication between the body – the realm of embodied purposes – and what we call the mind, the realm of intention (cf. Rappaport 1977). Although the specific intentions expressed in petitionary prayer are of course articulated ones, the underlying agenda is likely to be unacknowledged. Alice prays that God will control what she cannot, but conceives this as turning over responsibility to God. Larry prays, for example, for a miracle of healing, but in so doing is allowed to disrupt a church service in a spectacular fashion. The canonical language, as in earlier chapters, provides a medium through which embodied and potentially disruptive purposes may be formulated, with the result that the believer arrives at an adjustment between his or her desires and the demands of social existence.

This movement between embodied aims and intentions articulated in terms of the canonical language can occur only because of the ability of language to constitute an ongoing situation. As Larry and Alice tell their stories, they re-enact the central emotional motifs of their conversions. Larry disrupts his own narration, just as he disrupted the church service decades earlier. Alice dramatizes her conversion, replaying it in a way that both allows her to express her embodied aims and to do so within a framework that demonstrates that those aims remain ultimately under control. Her emotions are invoked to lend power to her narrative, but they do not disrupt the narrative to the extent that Alice is unable to continue.

Thus the conversion story, which is told in a conventionalized language that allows these believers to share their stories with an appreciative community, becomes in its telling an occasion for the manifestation of the embodied. It is this ability to use canonical language in a way that blends into metaphoric communication that makes possible the ritual communication between what we call the mind and the body.

6   Roles

In the previous chapter, I considered a problem that is central to an understanding of the relationship between intention and canonical language, that of how canonical language can be used to come to terms with the impulse to control. I suggested that the canonical language may be used to express an embodied purpose as the intention of God, with the result that the believer may attempt to control by giving up control. For some, the verbal practice of prayer may be an additional technique for the expression of unacknowledged purposes.

In this chapter I will consider another use of a narrative form to accomplish such an end; specifically, I will discuss narrative strategies of re-enactment. In these cases the believer recreates, on the level of performance, the conflict that motivated his or her conversion, in order to also re-enact his or her deliverance from that conflict. Thus, whereas believers in the previous chapter used verbal techniques of coming to terms with embodied aims, in this chapter the techniques depicted are more dramatic.[1] Both general styles, verbal and dramatic, are characterized by shifts between metaphoric and canonical communicative behaviors.

Jan: conversion and control of the body

Jan, who was in her mid-forties when I met her, was a woman I enjoyed interviewing. She talked freely and had a good sense of humor; we seemed to hit it off well. I mention this because I think the relationship she established with me is probably typical of many of her relationships: Jan is comfortable in interacting with others, warm and – perhaps especially – adaptable. I noticed this during the interview and I find signs of it throughout the transcript. Interactions between the two of us proceeded smoothly; consider the following, almost conspiratorial, exchange. Jan has been talking about the family she grew up in, and switches to discussing her own family. I have just met her teenage son, who appeared, with no explanation, in a dress:

JAN: and I think my <u>own</u> kids.......have
insecurities......but? I, I guess all? kids............#you
know=
INTERVIEWER: =right=
JAN: =that's the problem # EVERYBODY has them,   (5)
INTERVIEWER: right=
JAN: =MINE (p-) seem pretty to<u>gether</u>..............((voice
change, softer, like an aside)) {even though he was wearing
this dress}
INTERVIEWER: (ha) yeah well yeah, except for that one little   (10)
thing |(ha)|
JAN: |(yeah {that}) little aberration|
INTERVIEWER: (ha) u:m-
JAN: SO I- I mean uh- that's what I <u>tried to</u>....I TRIED TO
be more....I'm <u>much</u> more demonstrative.......|than I think   (15)
my family was|
INTERVIEWER: |{than your parents} uh huh|

This passage also touches on another theme that Jan emphasizes
repeatedly. This is that the family in which she grew up was not close, and
that she has tried to compensate for that by being especially close to her
sons:

JAN: and I think that u:m.......when my KIDS were growing
up.......I had very <u>definite</u> ide:as as
to.................u:m....#you know that I should <u>nurse</u>   (20)
them, #that I should <u>be</u> with them: that I shouldn't <u>work</u>
|that I|
INTERVIEWER: |uh huh|
JAN: should <u>take care</u> of them:....and do <u>everything</u>....for
them (ha) maybe ((telephone rings)) (it) you know I got that   (25)
a little EXAGGERATED (ha)

In a sense, Jan's style of interaction and her attempts to be close to her
sons can be seen as manifestations of the same underlying theme, that
being that Jan is sensitive to and adapts to the needs of others. The skills
that enable Jan to interact in a close and fluid manner with an interlocutor
are the same ones needed to sustain a close relationship with her teenage
sons.

Such skills, however, may entail certain liabilities. Jan says that her very
attentiveness to the needs of others has led, throughout her life, to not
being fully aware of her own needs:

INTERVIEWER: (ha) well may:be particularly in regard then to
your <u>mo:ther</u> you didn't want to be:..........what your
mo:ther........wanted you |to be|
JAN: |I didn't| want to be:......<u>walked on</u> in   (30)

life. . . . .|and you|
INTERVIEWER: |hm|
JAN: know wha:t?. . . . . .((dec)) <u>my sons walk all: over me</u> it's
<u>so</u> funny. . . . .'h I didn't want to <u>be:</u> the. . . .like #I always
thought of my mother as a#. . . . .<u>door</u>mat that we <u>wi:ped</u>   (35)
our <u>feet</u> on. . . .<u>you</u> know. . . .how you e<u>quate</u> that. . . .but
everybody took <u>adva:ntage</u> of her in my <u>family</u>. . . .my <u>fa:ther</u>
did. . . . .(ha) ((laugh sounds frustrated)) 'H and-
and everybody el:se did. . . .and then I <u>found</u> tha:t. . . .<u>and</u>
<u>I-</u> I: wasn't going to be that (way)   (40)
INTERVIEWER: uh huh
JAN: be that dependent. . . .and then I <u>found</u>
that. . . . . .I: do <u>everything</u> for my. . . . . .I <u>did</u>
everything for my ki:ds,

In the years after the birth of her first child, Jan reacted to these sorts of
frustrations by eating. She gained a great deal of weight and found that
she was unable to lose it again. A description of herself that Jan
formulated in another context, the reasons for the eventual break-up of
her marriage, also sheds some light on the emotional situation that may
have contributed to her weight problem:

JAN: I didn't have an IDENTITY?. . . .as a <u>self</u>. . . .my WHOLE   (45)
IDENTITY wa:s. . . .JOHN and Neil's MO:M and HUGH'S wife, THAT
was m- there was NO- 'H that was a <u>really big</u> thing to
me. . . .that there was <u>no</u> Jan, JAN |didn't exist|
INTERVIEWER: |you| you explicitly thought that |there is no|
JAN: |I EX|plicitly thought <u>I</u> DO NOT EXIST AS A PERSON, I   (50)
am <u>only</u> an apPENdage of 'h the <u>children</u> I'm their <u>mother</u> and
I'm <u>Hugh's</u> wife. . . .<u>I:</u> as an <u>individual</u> have no identity. . . .
INTERVIEWER: and that made you fee::l. . . . . .what-
dead?. . . .what <u>wor-</u> is there a <u>word</u> for how that made you
fee:l?. . . . . .#did it make you feel depressed# {did it make   (55)
you feel empty} did it make you feel <u>desolate</u>. . . . .{I
mean} do you re<u>mem</u>ber wha=
JAN: = #I'm trying to think,# wait a minute
no:w. . . . . .I (could) it was <u>only</u>
when I <u>recognized</u> that. . . .<u>lack</u> of identity. . . .   (60)
INTERVIEWER: uh huh?. . . .
JAN: #you know at the# <u>ti:me</u>. . . . . . . .I (s)- sorta saw that
and said okay you're <u>choosing</u> to <u>do</u>
thi:s. . . . . . .<u>to</u>. . . .de<u>VOTE</u> yourself to it. . . .and after I
di:d,. . . .I <u>realized</u> the ((voice change)) I think the word is   (65)
<u>emptiness</u> of it. . . .
INTERVIEWER: uh huh. . . .
JAN: you <u>ca:n't li:ve</u>. . . . . .off <u>someone else</u>. . . .
INTERVIEWER: uh huh. . . .
JAN: off <u>their identity</u>. . . .   (70)

INTERVIEWER: uh huh. . . .
JAN: you can't get your strokes because you're somebody's
wife. . . .
INTERVIEWER: uh huh
JAN: HEY HEY look I'm a good person I'm his wife (ha)   (75)
INTERVIEWER: uh huh. . . .
JAN: PAT me on the ba:ck. . . . .|u:m|
INTERVIEWER: |{uh huh}|. . . .
JAN: so it would be an emptiness and a lack
o:f. . . . .fulfillment. . . .|of GRATIFICATION| (80)
INTERVIEWER: |uh huh|. . . .uh huh. . . . .
JAN: and it became more and more OBVIOUS as the boy:s needed
me LESS, this was like in. . . .later elementary school
years. . . . . .THEY needed me |much less|
INTERVIEWER: |uh huh| (85)
JAN: and |what was|
INTERVIEWER: |uh huh|
JAN: what did I have left? and you know, I could look to
them growing awa:y and |leaving and|
INTERVIEWER: |uh huh| (90)
JAN: and I'd be a noth:ing. . . .I'd ha:ve noth:ing?. . . and I
had to do something about that

By Jan's testimony, she came to be so far out of touch with her own
identity that she felt she did not exist as an independent person. This is an
extreme version of being out of touch with her own purposes, and it
manifested itself in a feeling that her very body was not under her control.
She stresses that she felt she had no control over her eating, and when she
finally undertook to lose weight at any cost, it was above all the sense of
bringing one thing under her control that gave her hope. The following
passage does not explicitly draw on the content of the canonical language
of Evangelical Christianity; that is, Jan does not refer to this as a religious
process. However, note that the canonical language appears implicitly in a
number of ways in this passage: the episode is introduced as a turning point
that changed Jan's life around. It is described, as the conversion very often
is, in the language of rebirth. And finally, the very form of this story
partakes of the model of the conversion episode, an encounter that changes
a life:

JAN: but it WASN'T enough. . . . . . .a:nd I STILL was HEAVY I
still. . . . . .you know, ALL the things I wanted to be: were OUT
there, and I was hiding from wanting. . . .you know, #to- from #   (95)
be:ing that person. . . .'H so I went to a doctor. . . . . . .u:m
#for a regular physical checkup #. . . .and the doctor said to
me eh I mean this is so vivid because it's what I: think
changed my life around ((dec)). . . .
INTERVIEWER: uh huh. . . .   (100)

JAN: was he <u>said</u> to me:. . . .((voice change, nasal)) you
KNOW. . . .if you get in a CAR ACCIDENT. . . . . . .or anything
happens to you,. . . .YOU BETTER BE <u>close to DEATH</u> or I'm not
going to <u>touch</u> you, I wouldn't operate on you: you'll <u>die</u> on
the table you're so fat. . . . .|you know| (105)
INTERVIEWER: |uh huh|
JAN: and you're SO MUCH a big risk and <u>can't you</u> DO
something about this. . . .this is what. . . .my two hundred and
thirty five. . . .'h and it was like. . . .I <u>did</u> that. . . .and it
took a few months but on JANUARY ONE. . . . . .FIVE YEARS   (110)
ago. . . . . .what's #(are) we# in eighty three?=
INTERVIEWER: =uh huh=
JAN: =seventy eight. . . . . .I s:TARTED to do something
about it and it took me:. . . . . .I <u>still</u> haven't
finished. . . . . . . .but. . . . . .it it took me a <u>lo:ng</u>   (115)
<u>wa:y</u> (ha) down the road. . . .started. . . .<u>running</u> and then and
then I beg- I started <u>walking</u>. . . .and then I began to-. . . .to
run. . . .|a little you know, <u>jog</u>|
INTERVIEWER: |uh huh|
JAN: and stuff 'h and I began to lose <u>weight</u>,. . . .a:nd I   (120)
bega:n to think. . . . . . .if <u>I</u> can <u>control</u>
this. . . . .((voice change)) {if} I can
contro:l. . . .((voice change)) my <u>eating</u>,. . . . . .maybe I can
<u>control</u> other aspects of my life. . . .
INTERVIEWER: uh huh. . . . . . .   (125)
JAN: and that's when. . . .((higher pitch)) <u>a:ll</u> of me began to
<u>change</u> and- and then that's when:. . . . .((taps foot
loudly)) I beca:me. . . .able to say ((voice change)) <u>hey</u> Hu:gh
(ha). . . .'h there's a whole lot of <u>needs</u> I have. . . .you're not
mee:ting them,. . . .|U:H| (130)
INTERVIEWER: |{uh huh}|
JAN: ((mock shouting voice)) GUESS WHAT? (ha). . . .WE'VE GOT
SOME RE:AL PROBLEMS HERE and I::M NOT GONNA JUST STAND
AROUND ANYMORE. . . .I WANNA DO SOMETHING ABOUT IT ((voice
change)) you <u>kno:w</u>. . . .I started to <u>ru::n</u>. . . .I started- 'h   (135)
and #(as I could) lose the weight# then I could start <u>do:ing</u>
what I see- it's so <u>funny</u> I see of me- as me: (as a) <u>re:al</u>
<u>person</u> and like (it) was. . . .((voice change)) <u>hidden</u> in this
<u>fat</u> person. . . .
INTERVIEWER: uh huh   (140)
JAN: the <u>person</u> was <u>the:re</u> and they <u>couldn't</u> get <u>out</u>. . . .
INTERVIEWER: uh huh. . . .
JAN: and <u>NOW</u> they're <u>OUT</u>
INTERVIEWER: uh huh |(ha)|
JAN: |AND WATCH OUT WORLD| (145)

For Jan, the process of losing weight was one of gradually rediscovering
her ability to control aspects of her own life, and through this growing

ability, to discover her identity. This passage demonstrates something else as well, as do several of the passages above: Jan is an excellent storyteller. Her style of narration is noteworthy first of all for the heavy use of direct quotes, often acted with considerable dramatic flair.

In English the speaker may report the speech of another person directly, by quoting it, or indirectly. Indirect speech differs grammatically from direct speech in several ways. First of all, indirect speech is introduced with the subordinating conjunction "that" ("she said that A" vs "she said, 'A'"). More generally, indirect speech is grammatically oriented to the situation in which it is reported rather than the situation it reports. For example, in indirect speech verb tense will be determined by the present context rather than the context of the original utterance: "He said that he was not going to eat with us" vs "He said, 'I am not going to eat with you.'"[2] For the purposes of this argument, the significant difference between direct and indirect speech is that direct speech is more dramatic. It involves the speaker in playing a role and gives the speaker the opportunity to depict not only what was said but how it was said (Volosinov 1973). As noted in a recent article on the topic, "the more 'direct' varieties [of quotation] import features of the projected speech situation into the projecting one, to a greater extent than do the 'indirect' ones" (Rumsey 1990: 347).

Some of the people I interviewed exploit the possibilities of direct speech much more than others do; Jan is certainly one of those who excels in her use of this technique of reporting. Here, for example, Jan begins by quoting the doctor who told her she was overweight. Then she tells about her feelings from several years ago by quoting her admonitions to herself. She reconstructs the effects of this process upon her marriage by imitating herself arguing with her husband with a raised voice, thus conveying the urgency and anger with which she began to recognize what she calls her needs.

Another storytelling technique Jan uses here to not only recall but actually re-enact the past is her use of word stress and of the progression of motion words from "walk" to "run" to "jog" to emphasize the processual nature of her accomplishment. To recount a process from the past, she uses processual verbal formulations in telling her story.

Jan consistently blends past thoughts into present, as she does at lines 137–141, where she integrates her idea of a real person hidden inside a fat person into the framework of explaining how she lost the weight. Her narrative accomplishment here is particularly striking in that this idea – the real person inside the fat person – is itself embedded in another frame, for it begins as an aside as she starts but does not finish the statement at line 137. The tense returns to the present at line 143, where she announces her own birth out of the midst of her former overweight self. In other words, again here performance is recapitulating the story being told, for she tells about her emergence as her words themselves emerge from the frame in which they have been embedded.

The effect of these various techniques of narration is to recapitulate, on the level of performance of the narrative, the predicament that is described in the referential meaning of Jan's words. That is, one could say that Jan's story does not only recount her experience, it recreates it. In light of terminology I have suggested earlier, Jan's narrative constitutes an emotional and rhetorical situation that parallels the process of her weight loss. She not only uses various devices, such as direct quotation, to bring the story into the present, but works to recapitulate in the structure of her narrative the situation she found herself in five years previously (cf. Lévi-Strauss 1963). As she recounts the laborious process of starting to jog, her narration becomes laborious and processual. As she quotes her new attitude towards her husband (at lines 128–130), she enacts a conventional rhetorical figure that expresses what she did at the time, in that she literally "puts her foot down." As she tells of the emergence of the real Jan from underneath the fat, her phrase emerges out of the larger frame in which it had been embedded.

The image of herself being hidden within an overly large body exemplifies a theme that occurs repeatedly in this interview, Jan's inability to find herself. It appeared, for example, in her insistence that she lacked an identity in her marriage and that she put the needs of her family above her own. But perhaps most tellingly, this theme emerges in Jan's interactive and narrative styles. Interactively, as noted, Jan adjusts fluently and easily to her interlocutor. And the repeated use of direct quotation and other narrative techniques for manifesting the past in the present can be seen as indicative of the ease with which Jan takes on a role.

The "conversion" from overweight person to a person who is able to control her weight is explicitly concerned with this issue, that of finding herself, finding her own ability to control. In her discussion of her religious commitments, it is not surprising then that Jan returns to this theme. The first thing her religious commitment has given her, says Jan, is a greater acceptance of herself. Her discussion of this theme makes it clear that it is on the basis of her own feelings about her family that Jan has grasped God's acceptance:

JAN: ALL ALONG is HOW CAN?- you know....WHY would he LOVE me
and............you kno:w I'M- I'M just a NOTHING you kno:w
and I've made so many misTAKES and I....continue to; to DO
things WRO:NG and....a:nd stuff like that...........and it

was. . . .once I could. . . . . .believe that ((voice change,   (150)
breathy, higher)) Go:d lo:ves me, no matter what I did. . . .he
would always love me. . . .and. . . .realize that that's how I
felt about my: children. . . .no matter what they do I will
ALways love them, there's nothing they could do: to |destroy
that love| (155)
INTERVIEWER: |uh huh|
JAN: they could make me ANGRY. . . . .|and they|
INTERVIEWER: |uh huh|
JAN: could make me PUNISH them. . . .
INTERVIEWER: uh huh. . . .   (160)
JAN: but. . . .the love would be the:re. . . . . .and if the:y
asked for forgiveness or came seeking help, I would AL:WAYS
give it to them. . . .((voice change, higher)) and that's
EXA:CTLY what GO:D is saying to us. . . .|you know so then I
thought| (165)
INTERVIEWER: |uh huh|. . . .
JAN: if God loves me, h:ow can I not love
myself. . . . . .if GOD loves me how can I: refuse to love
me =
INTERVIEWER: = uh huh =   (170)
JAN: = what right do I have |to do that|
INTERVIEWER: |uh huh| uh huh
JAN: so I gra:dually bega:n, and I'm still, got a ways to
go, you know. . . .to accept myself. . . . .
INTERVIEWER: uh huh   (175)
JAN: a::nd to:. . . . . . . .feel that I was an okay person

Earlier Jan talked about her relationship to her children as related to
her own feeling of lack of identity. Here, however, she is able to use this
self-negating feeling as a basis for self-acceptance. Her strong sensation of
love for her own children is the model she uses to understand God's love
for her. Here, then, Jan is able to obtain what she has evidently always
wanted, closeness and acceptance. God becomes a substitute for her own
natal family, her husband, even her children, none of whom have accepted
Jan as she has accepted them. Note, however, that it is precisely her own
adaptability to her sons – a quality that she said earlier enabled them to
walk all over her – that provides the basis for her understanding of God
and his forgiveness. This overadaptability has not been changed through
Jan's religious experience, rather it has been placed within a frame where it
no longer causes as much conflict as it once did. Jan has always wanted the
kind of acceptance from others that she feels she offers to them, but she
has always been disappointed. Now, however, she has discovered that
acceptance in her relationship to God.

The second point that Jan emphasizes about her conversion is that it strengthened her ability to turn over responsibility. By this Jan means that throughout her life she has been troubled by trying to take responsibility for things that are not completely under her control, such as the safety of her sons.

INTERVIEWER: so #it was never a problem for you to love your
neighbor, # the problem was LOVING YOURSELF (ha)....
JAN: m:ore so yeah
INTERVIEWER: and that's......   (180)
JAN: a:nd and turning over responsibility.......
INTERVIEWER: uh huh=
JAN: =I: was always the one who thought I was responsible
for everything
INTERVIEWER: uh huh {yeah}   (185)
JAN: I mean..................people do: an- and everybody
does,..........and I: just took everything to HEART like
m-my husband something- he would bump into into
something?....and he'd turn and gla:re at me.......as if it
was my fault ((voice change, more urgent)) now- you- people   (190)
do that
INTERVIEWER: yeah
JAN: #I mean# even I DO THAT
INTERVIEWER: yeah
JAN: AND IT'S THE INSEN-I MEAN IT'S THE UH....INSECURE?   (195)
PERSON WHO....ABSO:RBS THAT AND SAYS ((dramatic voice
change, to whisper)) Go:d? it's RIGHT, |(you know)|
INTERVIEWER: |uh huh|
JAN: but that doesn't make any LOGICAL SENSE? so you REBE:L
against it   (200)
INTERVIEWER: uh huh
JAN: you kno:w....|but e:|
INTERVIEWER: |uh huh|
JAN: MO:tionally you feel, ugh......................((loud
exhalation, sounds frustrated)) BUT-.............THAT SENSE   (205)
OF RESPO:NSIBILITY for everything is- was much too big a
burden for me carry
INTERVIEWER: uh huh
JAN: and to give that to someone else 'h....for
example,...............when my so:n doesn't come home   (210)
((nervous laugh))....
INTERVIEWER: uh huh
JAN: and I'm terrified and I'm frightened and I'm a ca- I
ca-n't sleep when they're out you know I just kno:w when
they come home, I've gotten #LOTS BETTER by the older   (215)
one #....'h but when he was:....s:ixteen and seventeen
and....he #didn't show up on ti:me #,.............it ((dec))
HELPED ME SOMEwhat, it didn't ea:se i:t....TOTALLY (ha) and

I STILL PACE(D) the FLOOR. . . .'h but I didn't become TOTALLY
FRANTIC. . . .that HE:. . . .I could sa:y, I could PRAY TO GOD, I   (220)
HAD AN OUTLET, I could TALK to GO:D and ask him to bring him
home sa:fe. . . .
INTERVIEWER: uh huh
JAN: I COU:LD. . . .um:. . . . . .ga:in some measure of
peace,. . . . .| #even though| (225)
INTERVIEWER: |uh huh|
JAN: I had to # KEE:P DOING IT, you know,
INTERVIEWER: uh huh. . . . .
JAN: but I had a person, I had. . . .((voice change, higher)) a
person to turn to,. . . . .   (230)
INTERVIEWER: uh huh
JAN: in ti:mes when I was afrai:d,. . . . . .and he would
calm me down

Once again, Jan turns to an example from her family life to explain her
relationship to God. By praying, she is able somehow to relinquish some
of the responsibility she feels for the safety of her son, and therefore to
weather difficult times of worrying.

The performance of this passage allows further insight into Jan's
feelings. At lines 183–187, she explains her own ambivalent feelings about
feeling responsible for things that happen to members of her family.
Although she feels such responsibility, at the same time she realizes that it
is not "logical" to do so. It is significant that this ambivalence is clearly
reflected in certain aspects of how Jan speaks these lines. There is, first of
all, the slip at line 195, where she very probably starts to say that the
person (herself) who feels responsibility for another's misfortune is
insensitive rather than insecure. A possible interpretation of this slip,
which fits well with what is known about Jan in general, is that she feels
that she is being insensitive by saying – as she is doing – that it is not her
responsibility if her husband bumps into something. Another sign of Jan's
ambivalent identification with her stated position here is at line 197, where
she rather dramatically shifts her voice to directly quote her own thought:
yes, it is my fault. But she does not sustain the new, whispering voice
throughout the quote, rather she switches back to the noticeably loud
voice in which she has been narrating this entire episode. Further evidence
that she shifts from direct to indirect quotation in the middle of her phrase
is her wording. In direct quotation, one would expect to hear "God, that's
right." (And indeed this is the way my transcriber first recorded this line.)
But Jan definitely says "it's right," which is what she would have said if
the phrase had been introduced with a subordinating conjunction: "it's
the insecure person who says to himself that it's right." Finally, there is a
slip in verb tense at line 206; Jan intends to say that her sense of complete

responsibility is something she found hard to bear in the past. However, what she actually says first is that it is hard to bear in the present.

These performative features of the narrative at this point reinforce what Jan is explicitly saying, that she feels ambivalent about giving up responsibility for her family members' activities. Although Jan may conceive such a feeling of responsibility as a sign of how deeply she cares about her family, it must also be pointed out that this is an omnipotent style of thinking. That is, to think that she is responsible for her husband's bumping into something is to attribute a great deal of power and control to herself. Thus one may say that there is an unacknowledged aim here, that of being omnipotent, of controlling what happens to her family members.

It is interesting to notice that Jan tends to feel she has no control over herself, as in her eating, but finds it reasonable on some level that she controls her husband's movements. Unfortunately, it is not possible to go beyond this, on the basis of the available data, and say anything about the source of this paradoxical conviction. What is most relevant here is simply that in prayer Jan is turning over to God the responsibility for her son's safety. That is, she is giving up some of her own aim to be omnipotent to God. This is a strategy similar to the one used by Alice and Larry, for her God is made the channel of the embodied purpose.

More generally, however, although Jan deals with problems that are similar to those of the believers discussed in the previous chapter, the techniques she uses to come to terms with these problems are different from the ones discussed there. Two themes run throughout Jan's narrative: she has been a person who does not accept herself and who has attended first to the needs of others rather than herself. Both the process of changing her body through weight loss and the act of making a religious commitment are oriented around these themes. One can see in her very style of storytelling, however, that in spite of Jan's conviction that she is doing better in these areas, she remains a person who seeks to adjust to the situation, and who retains much of the ambivalence she says she has left behind her. Her interactional style, her heavy use of direct quotation, and her recapitulation of omnipotent wishes in her present discourse are aspects of style that support the conclusion that Jan has not changed much. There are other indications of this as well. For example, Jan mentions that she likes her present job because its flexibility and location make it possible for her to continue to care for her sixteen-year-old son in the way she wants to. She mentions as an example leaving work to fetch and deliver her son's homework on mornings he has forgotten to bring it to school.

The interview shows how Jan has learned to manage habits that got out of hand and led to a situation that was threatening to her very sense of existence. She is, at least at the time of the interview, able to sustain a balance between awareness of her own purposes and her tendency to respond only to the needs of others. The analysis has shown how Jan uses canonical language to express unacknowledged purposes such as the desire for total acceptance or for omnipotence, thereby obviating expressing these purposes in ways that are more destructive to Jan and the people around her.

George, an unfaithful husband

I will now turn to a second subject whose interview manifests similar themes. In rough outline, the story George (who was in his early sixties when I spoke to him) told me went like this: George's father, who died when George was twenty-six years old, was a committed Christian and a firm person. That is, George depicts his father as a man who had strong opinions on things and shared those opinions with his son. George emphasizes that he and his father had many disagreements, but insists that they did not fight with one another. Rather, for the most part George tried to bow to his father's wishes, for he admired the older man tremendously. Thus, for example, George had given up Christianity by the time he entered college, but he had never directly confronted his father with this fact.

After college George married his high school sweetheart, but after three children and seven years of marriage he struck up an affair with a co-worker. He eventually left home and decided to divorce his wife. The relationship with the co-worker also broke up, and thereafter George embarked upon a period in which he dated many different women. However, on a visit to his family George was shocked when the youngest of his children did not recognize him. He was troubled, and seeing this, his ex-wife recommended he go and speak to a minister.

George did so, and the minister asked him "where he stood with God." George answered that he did not believe in God, to which the minister responded that perhaps he should give that position some thought. George left the pastor's office with a Christian book and, after some days of debating with himself the existence of God, decided to pray to God and ask his forgiveness. Upon doing so he was flooded with a profound feeling of forgiveness; he refers to this as a "road to Damascus type experience."

Having thus been converted to Christianity, George decided that he should put his life in order. He had already proposed to a woman he had been dating, and he decided to go and tell this news to his ex-wife. However as he stood before her he found that he was physically unable to speak the message he had come to convey, and instead asked her to remarry him. She consented, and they have been married ever since that time.

Two themes from this capsule summary seem worth pursuing in this context. First, George is concerned with the issue of his father's control over his life. Many of George's comments testify to such a concern; perhaps the strongest evidence here is George's insistence that he never fought with his father:

```
GEORGE: 'h so uh. . . .it was (w) we never fought no we never
ever fought ((strong emphasis)). . . . . . . . . . . . . . . . . . . .'h              (235)
ABOUT ANYTHING. . . . . . .
INTERVIEWER: huh ((high tone then dropping off)). . . . . . . .
GEORGE: 'h uh:. . . . . . . . . . . . . . . . . .'h women hav-. . . . . .((voice
changes until end of sentence)) girls, and women have
played a very important part in my life and uh ((clicking          (240)
sound)). . . .I uh I was very fond of one Catholic girl. . . .
INTERVIEWER: uh huh. . . . . . . . . . . .
GEORGE: ((clicking sound)) a:nd he just said
{George,. . . . . . . . . .it'd be better for you if you would}
{{knock it off there's lotsa girls and I know Cissy's a          (245)
nice girl but I think it would work out |better|}}
INTERVIEWER: |uh huh|
GEORGE: {I didn't fi:ght about it I- I accepted it}
```

The second theme here has to do with the prominence in this story of George's inability to speak when he visited his ex-wife to tell her about his impending marriage. In light of this, I was interested to notice that there are a number of moments in the interview where he has a milder version of the same problem. There are four places where George breaks down as he speaks and is unable for a moment to say what he evidently intends.[3] The first of these occurs as George recalls his father:

```
GEORGE: he uh # he was not a wishy washy man # he was
a. . . .determined he was a typical                              (250)
wasp. . . . . . . .he:. . . . . . . .belie:ved that he had a pur:pose
((voice begins breaking here)). . . .in life {he} taught me a
lot of. . . . . .very wonderful things that I've later discovered
were. . . . . .# not original? ((stop voice breaking)) he didn't
SAY they were, #. . . .but # you know #                          (255)
INTERVIEWER: uh huh
GEORGE: maybe if we have time later on I'll. . . .{I can tell
you about some of them}
INTERVIEWER: # no go ahead tell me #. . . .|tell me one
(indistinguishable)|                                             (260)
GEORGE: |OKAY ONE| of them I':d I'd never forget is
```

the. . . . . . .the i- is this <u>sho:rt</u>, thing. . . . .'h I cannot
do everything but I can do something. . . .I- I. . . . .am but
one?. . . . .{but I (am one)?} ((voice breaking,
weeping))

In all of the following examples, I have classified the situation as a "temporary inability to speak" not because of the presence of any particular marker, but rather because these instances each somehow convey the impression of extreme difficulty in speaking. In this case, this impression arises out of the stutters at lines 261, 262 and 263, the moderately long pauses at lines 262 and 264, and the breaking voice. The latter interferes with speech most thoroughly at line 264, where the listener gets a strong impression that it is very difficult for George to say "but I am one" (if that is indeed what he says; the transcription is uncertain).

The second case of "inability to speak" also occurs in connection with a discussion of George's father:

INTERVIEWER: |oh <u>really</u>| (265)
GEORGE: |the- the| one of the most rema:rkable interviews
we('d) ever had in our life. . . . .'h my f- <u>mother</u> was
awa:y. . . . . . .looking after an <u>aunt</u> in <u>Florida</u> ((clicking
sound)). . . . . . . .and uh we were ⧣ just <u>riding</u>?
around, ⧣. . . . . .which was: a custom in those <u>days</u> that was one   (270)
ah th- 'h. . . .ways you H:ADDA <u>being</u>. . . . ⧣ <u>alone</u> with
somebody ⧣. . . .|'H|
INTERVIEWER: |uh huh|
GEORGE: and uh:. . . .he said George?. . . . .((voice change))
I- he said <u>I</u>: know you're not a Christian {{now}}. . . . .   (275)
INTERVIEWER: uh huh
GEORGE: and uh. . . . .but ((dec)) {I'm con<u>vinced</u> you <u>will</u>?
be}. . . . . .((slowly, voice breaking))
INTERVIEWER: huh ((high tone, then dropping
off)). . . . .   (280)
GEORGE: 'h {and when you are you'll be different} ((speech
very soft, breathy – no support from diaphragm))

Here, as noted in the transcription, George's trouble in speaking culminates in the phrase of line 281, which sounds as if it were being forced out with no support behind it. Leading up to this phrase, George's voice again begins to break and the volume of his speech drops noticeably.

The third example of this phenomenon occurs in the interview as George recalls a visit with his children after he had divorced his wife:

GEORGE: and uh one of the first times (I-) we had uh chi:ld
visitation {you know}
INTERVIEWER: uh huh
GEORGE: oh I <u>REALLY</u> I mean I KNOW HELL ON EARTH. . . .'h I mean

I REALLY KNOW HELL ON EARTH,. . . . .((dramatic change
in tone between earth and two)) {two things especially stand
out in my:. . . .mind. . . . . .one time I came home and our
daughter didn't know me} {{I was just a
stranger}}. . . . . .((clicking sound)). . . . . .oh I tell you   (290)
boy that really shook me up. . . . . . .
INTERVIEWER: {uh huh}. . . . .
GEORGE: she was just a little {{little thing you know}}. . . .
((voice almost breaking))
INTERVIEWER: uh huh uh huh
GEORGE: 'h and then. . . .another time or maybe the sa:me visit   (295)
I:: don't know. . . . .'h uh my so:n said. . . .who
was. . . . . . .five six said. . . . .((slight tone change))
Daddy aren't you ever {coming home,}. . . . .
INTERVIEWER: uh huh
GEORGE: 'H. . . . .{I mean} ((breaks up during   (300)
I mean, then voice changes)) TALK ABOUT A SHAKE UP. . . .oh
brother 'H. . . . .((voice
change)) but uh. . . . . .you know Reno. . . . . .you'll never
know this I suppose unless I tell you, but Reno is just very
full of very attractive. . . . . . .and very available. . . . .   (305)
INTERVIEWER: uh huh. . . .
GEORGE: women

Here George experiences noticeable difficulty in speaking at lines 289–
290 and 293, but I would not classify this difficulty as an inability to speak.
The reason for this is that while the softness of voice and the breaking
voice that occur here are in some sense dysfluent (Hill 1990b), neither of
these features gives the impression of a breakdown, an inability to speak.
However, at lines 300 and 302 pauses of such length occur that they must
be labeled lapses (Moerman 1988). These, together with a breaking voice,
again indicate an inability to speak. This impression is strengthened by the
drastic shift of subject at line 303, following a lapse of 3.5 seconds, which
indicates that George simply cannot go on with the topic of his visit with
his children.[4]

The final instance of a temporary inability to speak occurs at the crucial
moment in the narration of George's conversion experience:

GEORGE: 'h and finally ((exhales)). . . . . . . .at no:on 'h on
the third day[5]. . . . . .I was re-. . . .I
was. . . . . . . .thinking about it and then all of a sudden I   (310)
just felt I should pra:y. . . .and I. . . .((voice begins to
break)) my prayer went like this. . . .((voice change, louder))
dear God. . . . .if you
exist. . . . . 'h ((dec)) let
me kno:w that you exist {and that you can forgive me}   (315)

In this passage, there is again a lapse (line 314) that is too long to be classified as a dysfluency and instead must be seen as a temporary inability to speak. As in earlier examples, the breaking voice and soft volume are also present here.

The conventional interpretation of a temporary inability to speak would be that "George is emotional" and that he is overcome by the emotion of remembering these events as he tells about them. For several reasons, I agree with Hill (1990a) that this is an inadequate interpretation. First, it does not clarify anything. Emotion can make one eloquent as well as inarticulate, and there are several emotional moments in the interview where George doesn't break down. Furthermore, to say "emotion is interfering" and leave it at that is merely a crude device to avoid analysis by tracing the inability to speak to something that is presumably outside the social scientific purview. I do not deny that emotion is centrally involved in George's temporary inability to speak, but I do deny that this is a sufficient explanation. What emotion is involved here and why should it lead to an inability to speak?

It is surely significant that all of George's temporary inabilities to speak occur in episodes that lead up to direct quotation of the speech of people close to him (or in one case, his own earlier speech). Why should each of these stories be set up around a direct quotation? And in each case, the actual inability to speak is associated with the direct quotation, another rather enigmatic regularity.

A paper by Greg Urban (1989) suggests a line of thought which may lead to some insight into what is going on here. Urban (1989: 29) refers to the "I" which occurs in direct quotation as the "anaphoric I," for the reason that this "I" does not refer to the present speaker but rather to some other speaker identified in an earlier clause. As noted earlier, the anaphoric I engages the speaker, to some extent, in role play. (The anaphoric I that engages the speaker in role play is also referred to by Urban as the "de-quotative I.") Urban in fact argues that the anaphoric I is the basis for such developments as a theatrical tradition.

From this perspective, the question becomes "why does George blow his lines" (just as he did when he could not say what he had planned to say to his ex-wife)? His doing so is especially mysterious in light of the fact that these stories are all set up to peak (Hill 1991) around a direct quotation; in this sense George is not only blowing his lines, he is putting himself in a position to blow his lines. There are two somewhat opposed possibilities here, and I am going to suggest that both contain an element of truth. The first possibility is that breaking down at these moments is a strategic means of presenting himself as an emotional man with strong feelings about his intimates. By being unable to speak George is communicating that he is sensitive, that he loved his children in spite of what he did to them, etc.

Alternatively, one could recall that direct quotation is, in Goffman's (1986) term, a frame within speech in which the speaker is temporarily standing in for someone else. And that means that the speaker temporarily suppresses certain aspects of him or herself in favor of expressing aspects of another person. Urban (1989: 36) phrases this point as follows:

> The imitated discourse of the other is no longer simply subject to whim. It is also subject to the control that the imitated other exercises over the speaker, since modifying or overturning the words of another is understood with the awareness that they *are* the words of another. The anaphoric "I" ... brings into one's discourse the real control that the imitated others have over one.

From this perspective, George's inability to speak would be generated out of an initial resistance to "the real control that imitated others have over" him. Lest this seem a somewhat tenuous interpretation, recall that the events of George's life demonstrate very clearly that at some times he has resented the strictures placed upon him by those closest to him.

I suggest that both of these possibilities have some validity because I do not think it is possible to clearly delineate George's purposes on the basis of this interview. It is possible, however, to conclude that he has some strongly ambivalent feelings about, on the one hand, independence and, on the other, commitment and dependence. George notes that his mother often criticized her husband for being out nearly every night; George's father was very active in the community and was involved in a wide range of civic activities. But, says George, he himself never resented his father's absences.

George describes his father as a man who was able to balance considerable independence with a nearly perfect fulfilling of family commitments, but George discovered that his own attempts to achieve these contradictory goals ended up making him miserable. Thus George's narrative style tells us the same thing that his story tells us, namely that he struggles with the conflict between his desire for independence and his desire for commitment to a strong family life. What the instances of quoted speech share with the episode in which he cannot speak the words he had intended to his wife is that both involve the conflict of these two motives. In the instances of quoted speech, George seems to convey both his commitment and his resentment thereof. And when he cannot tell his wife that he has asked another woman to marry him, George feels a conflict between his obligations to the family he helped to create overriding his desire to escape them.

Recall now that the original conversion event itself was also presumably generated out of an impasse between George's desire for independence and the constraints imposed by his family. George had been trying to escape those constraints but in doing so he arrived at a paralysis of action that parallels his paralysis of speech. As with the utterance, the paralysis is a noticeable impasse, where George stands suspended between two models of what to be. But also as with the utterance, the impasse is overcome by submission to the authority that was temporarily resisted.

George's situation parallels that of the believers discussed previously in that the central emotional ambivalence that by his testimony animated the conversion, in his case that of a desire to simultaneously escape from and honor his family commitments, persists in the conversion narrative itself. And, as has been the case with other believers discussed here, the canonical language comes to serve as the means whereby George may formulate his unacknowledged aims and thereby forge a livable compromise. To conform to the upright Christian example set by his father is, for some reason, not possible for George until he conceives such behavior as mandated not by his own father but rather his father above. As was the case for Jean and for several other believers discussed here, a form of behavior that is not possible in a familial context becomes possible in a religious context.

Drama and constitutive communication

The two cases considered here can be usefully considered as case studies in role playing. In both narratives, the believer utilizes stylistic devices that evoke, and in a literal sense even reconstitute, the emotional conflict that led up to the conversion. Both believers act out that conflict and their deliverance from it.

What is true of all the believers discussed in this book is perhaps especially clear in these two cases: Jan and George use a language that always embraces two levels of communication. The words that describe their experience also link that experience to a transcendent level. But through the actual use of language, through various aspects of their skillful performance, something much more profound happens. Believers' significant experiences both of conflict and of deliverance from that conflict are not only described in the narrative, they are invoked, and to some extent even relived. Here, then, the canonical language is connected to experience in a way that goes far beyond a cognitive linkage. The canonical language is invested with meaning not in the narrow sense of cognitive meaning but in the full sense of "meaningfulness." A direct link is forged between experience and canonical language, a link that may enable the expression of heretofore inaccessible desires at the same time as it reaffirms the significance of faith.

7   Against a theory of volition

Bronislaw Malinowski (1954), in a classic anthropological discussion of magic, pointed out that in any society it is precisely those activities in which social actors face the greatest uncertainty that tend to take the form of ritual. Thus, to use one of his examples, Trobriand Islanders practice no magic in association with lagoon fishing, an activity that is safe and reliable because it depends upon the effective method of poisoning the fish in calm waters. On the other hand, "extensive magical ritual" (1954: 31) is practiced in conjunction with the dangerous and uncertain activity of deep sea fishing. Malinowski extended his observation to cover less pragmatic activities as well. Existential uncertainties such as the nature of death are also likely to be dealt with through some form of ritual. The mechanism here is the same as that involved in fishing; in junctures of uncertainty, the formulas of ritual offer reassurance and a feeling of certainty.

This point can be rephrased in terms of the terminology I have used in this book. When members of a society must go beyond the boundaries of the everyday, the predictable, the understandable, they exit the realm of the referential. Ritual may be construed as an attempt to extend control beyond these boundaries, to establish certainty precisely where life seems least certain. How this actually takes place in different societies probably depends on what is common sense and what is mysterious in those places; in particular, some authors have suggested that the functioning of ritual may be tied to the linguistic ideology in a society.[1] The extended example considered in this book can be seen in this light: In the ritual of the conversion narrative in our own society believers seek to control the uncertain through using canonical language to formulate purposes that might otherwise take shape as mysterious and discomforting disturbances of communication.

These observations on ritual and uncertainty can be inverted to yield an interesting question: If it is true that ritual occurs in the face of uncertainty, then it is legitimate to ask – when confronted with a ritual – what sort of social uncertainty does this ritual address? Specifically, the question I want to bring up here is that of the wider social context of the conversion ritual. I want to argue that the conversion ritual – like a number of other prominent rituals in our society – is a response to contradictions entailed in our common sense, particularly certain contradictions entailed in our conception of volition. And I am not unaware, as I pose this question, of an ironic fact: this book itself, in offering its own explanation of these contradictions, can be considered as a rival discourse to that of the conversion.

The most important implication of this irony, as I see it, is the danger that any overarching social scientific theory of volition – which will necessarily be formulated to some extent in the terms of our common-sense assumptions – will in the end simply reproduce in a new form the mysteries of previous discourses on volition. For this reason I argue against any theory of *how* persons are able to change their own social circumstances, and maintain that for now the most productive approach to this sort of question is to observe and explain specific instances of volitional behavior.

Essentialism in our common sense

The American, and generally Western, valuation of freedom and the individual means on one level that variations in behavior and thought are tolerated, conformity is not valued, and so on. But no society, of course, escapes a certain level of stricture: A society is in its very essence communication, and communication occurs only through some kind of shared system of assumptions. Thus if a society tolerates wide variations in substantive values, behaviors, and so on, one can expect to find consensual assumptions in some other level of social life, for without shared assumptions on some level, no communication is possible.

I have suggested that in our society an important level of shared assumptions is a series of largely unquestionable propositions about persons, language and interaction that I have referred to loosely as the character and intention system, a part of our common sense. I now want to take some time to expand and tie together my account of those portions of this system that are most relevant to an understanding of the conversion narrative.

Much of the character and intention system – and indeed of our common sense considered more broadly – can be understood as the entailments, in different realms, of a single underlying approach to comprehending social reality, an approach I will call essentialism (Popper 1957). This underlying approach has already been mentioned in discussing the referential ideology of language; in the case of language, what are essentialized in our common sense are meanings. But this essentializing approach extends beyond lanuage; it may be seen as an expression of a fundamental assumption used to order social reality in Western societies. Members of such societies tend to comprehend a wide range of psychological and social processes by positing "thinglike" essences – like the meaning of words – that orchestrate those processes behind the scenes.

Consider, for example, ideas about "mind."[2] Utterances are understood to refer to unseen entities that are the true content of language, entities such as ideas, feelings, and so on. An utterance merely gives public form to a separable thought or feeling that takes shape prior to its being expressed in words. Thus, for example, one may say "that's not what I meant" when one's utterance has been interpreted in a way that is incompatible with the instigating thought.

Thus one can see a direct connection between how the meaning of utterances is thought to occur in this society and our conception of mind. It is precisely because we think of utterances as carrying a referential essence around with them, regardless of context, that we may conceive of mind as the source and location of such essences. In our common-sense understanding of things, the mind occupies the body in precisely the way that meaning occupies an utterance; both are non-corporeal essences organizing the concrete manifestations we actually encounter in the world, people, and utterances.

Ideas about intentions are also, of course, closely linked to ideas about meaning. Philosophers such as Grice (1957), for example, have argued for a significant link between meaning and intention. Thus the essentialist framework for explaining meaning can also be seen to organize the common-sense understanding of intention that was described in the introduction. Minds are volitional centers that direct action on the basis of conscious and specifiable intentions. The mind reflects upon various courses of action, chooses one in light of the overall situation, and then acts. In this way the justification of action is reified and posited as a "thing" much like a meaning or a mind; we call this thing an intention.

The other term that has played an important role in the argument here is identity. Identity too is usually understood in essentialistic terms, as the coherent core of individuality (Erikson 1956). Identity is usually conceived as something that is brought into a situation by a person, and which shapes the flow and outcome of that situation. In this view identity is, like meaning and intention, an aspect of the mind; identity is thus something that exists outside of the different social contexts in which it is observed.

Throughout this book I have attempted to avoid reasoning from the premises of the character and intention system. I simply am not convinced there is any particularly good evidence for the common-sense model of language and the person. The essentialistic entities posited in this system do not reflect underlying realities but rather are an indication of how important it is in our society for there to be little doubt or question about the nature of social life. Processes are too ephemeral and unanchored, in our view; it is for this reason that we reconceive certain basic social processes as objects such as meanings, minds, intentions, and identities.

Because the very possibility of our society rests upon the consensus of the character and intention system, it is difficult for us to reason or even talk about a view of human life that contravenes elements of this consensus. This means that those aspects of human experience that belie the common-sense view will seem particularly threatening and mysterious. Such attitudes can be observed in our society in reactions to mental and emotional illness.

Mental illness and common sense

The existence of what we call mental and emotional illness is a threat to a principle that must remain unquestionable: human beings are by nature creatures with coherent intentions. The essence of human activity is to act according to intentions. This is what human beings do by nature, they are *defined* as volitional creatures. But the very core of what we call mental illness is behavior that is ambiguously intentional, and is therefore compromised volitionally. As psychologist David Shapiro (1981: 5) has written:

Some impairment of autonomy ... is intrinsic to all psychopathology. Every condition of psychopathology is characterized by modes of action that in one way or another comprise or distort normal volitional processes.

The sorts of things that are taken as indicative of mental disorders – fugue states, incoherent speech, uncontrolled movement, compulsions, extremely potent affective states – are all ambiguously intentional in the terms of the character and intention system.[3] That is, these actions cannot be construed as a part of a socially recognizable project. Those who are "crazy" are not even held to our communal standards of legality. They are in fact not fully acknowledged members of the community because they cannot be depended upon to produce intentional – that is, construable – behavior. The point is precisely that these people act outside the social order, and thereby forfeit their full membership in our community. They are excluded because they provide evidence that a central principle of our common sense is untrue: the principle that human beings act in pursuit of coherent projects must not be threatened.

My understanding of conversion narratives is predicated on the observation that human beings in fact do not always act in pursuit of coherent projects. That is, I hold that human beings often do not act in the prototypical sense of intentionality in that their behavior is often not construable as reflecting a coherent project. More accurately, human behavior may be construed in this way only with considerable social co-operation, by ignoring certain aspects of behavior, and so on. There is, in other words, an effective social conspiracy to maintain our particular outlook on volition, the illusion that behavior is preponderantly intentional.

When this illusion cannot be maintained, those involved will experience profound discomfort. Whatever the specific problem, it is a cause of suffering to the one who exhibits ambiguously intentional behavior and/or to those around her. Unlike much physical illness, mental illness is regarded as shameful. Thus people attempt to avoid producing the sorts of behavior that might be seen as indicative of mental illness. Social pressure – which may often be felt as the actor's own confusion, guilt, etc. – builds and creates pressure to restore the appearance of coherence. As Malinowski would predict, in this situation of social contradiction, of the undeniable presence of that which common sense denies, rituals are elaborated to restore the proper order. The conversion narrative is an example of a ritual that allows an actor to reconfigure his rogue aims and to channel them into a socially acceptable format, the language of Evangelical Christianity.

In this way, aspects of communicative behavior that index ambivalent purposes may be refashioned into the expression of coherent intentions. The substantive chapters of this book have offered a number of examples of how this can happen. These examples have demonstrated that conver-sion stories allow their narrators to formulate unacknowledged purposes in terms of the canonical language. Such a process has two implications: First, it may entail a sense of self-transformation because purposes that have contributed to incoherent behavior, behavior that does not harmo-nize with self-conception, may be formulated in terms of the canonical language. Second, the reformulation of previously metaphoric communi-cations in terms of the canonical language may give that language a level of experiential meaning (Lakoff 1987) that forms the basis for the subject's increased commitment to the language.

I have tried to show how these exchanges come about through shifts between referential and constitutive communicational behaviors. At this point it is worthwhile to review and summarize the effects of such shifts in the narratives presented in earlier chapters.

In the study of Jean, I showed how the idea of "connection" – a term Jean uses to refer to what might less idiosyncratically be called intimacy – is a central problem manifesting itself in various aspects of her work and social life. The narrative itself provides considerable evidence that "connection" is impossible for Jean in certain contexts, above all in the context of her family. In her family of origin, connection raises the spectre of absorption into a whole that threatens her sense of a separate identity.

Rather than saying that Jean wishes to avoid connection, though, it is more accurate to say that her feelings about connection are strongly ambivalent. It is at once that which she most desires and most dreads. She has found in her religious life a context in which she can express her profound desire for connection without experiencing attendant feelings of engulfment. Thus the language of connection to God, and the idea of being a member of God's family, both allows her to express purposes that she fiercely denies – and that clearly influence her speech behavior – and to understand God's word as a language that speaks directly to her deepest needs.

Jean's level of fluency varies considerably during the interview; dysfluencies and other aspects of prosody indicate a higher level of agitation while discussing her family than while discussing her religious life. Jean's feelings about her family are, in mitigated form, present in her narrative as she discusses her family. The language of "connection to God" can be seen as an aspect of canonical language that, in the presence of the disturbing feelings that have been evoked by Jean's discussion of her family, is used to placate and control those feelings. That is, the conversion narrative provides an opportunity for Jean to reformulate metaphoric behaviors in terms of the canonical language and thereby to articulate her unacknowledged aim of "connection." The canonical language thus comes to both constitute and refer: this language formulates Jean's unacknowledged aims while at the same time linking her to a social group that accepts and values these formulations.

The fact that the canonical language both constitutes and refers enables aspects of that language to effect a transformation between embodied aims and articulated intentions. Such a process may be observed in some form in all of the cases discussed in this book. Jim, for example, "breaks through" (Hymes 1981) an overall style of intellectualization – and thereby creates himself as the sort of person he aspires to be – in moments of narrating his most spiritual experiences. In spite of Jim's realization that he wants to express his emotions, he is unable to do so. The very intellectual powers that allow him to accurately discern his own unacknowledged purposes also serve to thwart those purposes in practice by rendering him an object of intellectual scrutiny to himself. However, this aim *is* realized in moments of using the canonical language. These moments are, as with Jean, sites of exchange between an ongoing, emotion-charged situation and the transcendent referents carried by the canonical language. In such moments the believer learns to connect an unacknowledged aim with some aspect of the canonical language, thereby expressing that which has heretofore been troubling and at the same time feeling the inexpressible power associated with the canonical language.

In discussing the stories told by Larry and Alice, I stressed the means whereby an intention articulated in terms of the canonical language – for example, "turning things over to God" – could express purposes that, in a more embodied form, might lead to considerable disruption. This analysis demonstrates the claim that the articulation of formerly embodied aims may entail a compromise that allows the believer to express unacknowledged aims in a manner that avoids significant social disruption. My analysis, however, extends beyond the claim that the canonical language may allow the articulation of an embodied aim. I also seek to show how this can happen. Such articulation happens through the believer's performance of the conversion narrative, because in this performance, in various ways, troublesome aspects of the believer's experience are invoked and tamed through placing them in a religious context.

My final cases, those of Jan and George, offer particularly clear examples of the constitution of the central conflict underlying the conversion, for in both these cases the conflict is re-played in the form of a drama. That is, the performance of these narratives makes clear what is true for all of the narratives I have discussed, that telling about conflicts experienced in the past offers an opportunity to re-enact those conflicts in the present. This re-enactment takes the form of metaphoric communicational behaviors, as for example with George's lapses in speech when he must give voice to the intentions of others.

But the practice of re-enactment works two ways. In addition to providing the possibility to act out an enduring conflict, the narrative may allow the believer to act out his delivery from that conflict. Just as verbal techniques make manifest the conflict, they make manifest its solution in terms of a canonical image that allows the believer to formulate an unacknowledged aim. The important point here is not that the efficacy of the canonical image is *recalled* in the conversion narrative, rather that efficacy is *experienced* in the narrative. Ongoing unacknowledged aims are formulated in terms of canonical images, images that refer and become *constitutive* through the performance of the narrative.

A comparison: the conversion and dynamic psychotherapy

I have argued that the conversion narrative is a response to contradictions in the common-sense understanding of volition, intention, etc., contradictions that are felt by subjects as confusion, guilt, and fear in the face of their own behavior. Of course, these sorts of feelings may be addressed in other ways than by having a conversion. The most culturally prominent means of addressing such feelings are the various forms of psychotherapy. If it is true that the practices of psychotherapy address themselves to the same contradictions mediated by the conversion, one should be able to observe parallels between these two social forms.

Although psychotherapy itself is worthy of extensive study, it will be useful in this context for me to make some general comments about this practice. I will confine my comments to the form of psychotherapy with which I have most experience, that being dynamic, insight-oriented therapy based in the work of Freud.[4] In dynamic psychotherapy, an actor who has begun to experience "symptoms," in essence to produce ego-alien behaviors, seeks relief through a process of applying language to her experience. A therapist attends closely to the communicational behavior of the patient, looking in particular for what I have called constitutive practices such as metaphors, slips of the tongue, stylistic regularities, and so on.

In sorting out the communicational behavior of the patient, most forms of dynamic therapy rely above all on a constitutive communicative process called the transference, the developing relationship between the therapist and the patient. It is assumed that the patient will begin to exhibit his symptoms in the context of the therapeutic relationship itself, and in particular that the sorts of patterns that are disrupting his relationships in the outside world will begin to show themselves in the relationship between patient and therapist.

This expectation is a logical one. If indeed the patient consistently lands in a particular social situation outside of therapy, one must assume such regularities occur because of some consistent behavior on the part of the patient. And if such behavior is really consistent, it should eventually appear in the therapeutic relationship as well. If it does, the treatment is greatly facilitated, for the therapist then has an example of the patient's problematic behaviors occurring right before her eyes. She can point out to the patient when he is behaving in a manner that has perpetuated the problems that brought him into therapy in the first place.

These sorts of interpretations, which are regarded by many practicing therapists as among the most effective sort of interventions available in the therapeutic process, conform to the model of shifts between the metaphoric and canonical communicational behaviors. The transference is what I have called a metaphoric process because it is activity that is initially opaque to interpretation; specifically, the transference is a pattern in the communicational behavior of patient and therapist (Crapanzano

1981). When some aspect of that pattern is labeled, a previously meta-phoric phenomenon is captured in the canonical language of the psychotherapeutic system. (Of course, in this case the enduring and transcendent aspects of the canonical language are likely to be borne by the notion that the psychotherapeutic system is scientific.) The result of this is the same sort of thing that happens in the conversion, an aspect of the constitutive is brought into the referential, and the boundaries of the articulable thereby change. At the same time, the efficacy of the therapist and the language she uses is demonstrated to the patient through the attendant generation of a sense of meaning, and commitment to the therapeutic system is thereby strengthened.

Although the theoretical frameworks used by dynamically oriented psychotherapists vary widely, it is likely that whatever particular form that framework takes, it will include the idea of the dynamic unconscious. That is, the efficacy of the therapy will be traced to a mysterious power that is invisible and transcends full understanding. The presence of such a mysterious power is typical of ritual; the efficacy of the ritual is traced to what I will call an "opacity." In explicitly religious rituals, of course, this opacity takes shape in the idiom of the supernatural.

Ritual, by its very nature, addresses itself to paradoxes and contradictions within a social order, to the socially generated impasse, to the juncture where cultural resources are insufficient to embrace reality. The workings of ritual, therefore, are always mysterious, dependent upon mechanisms that are opaque in terms of the conventions of the social order. I am arguing, then, that in both conversion narratives and dynamic psychotherapy, the emergence of embodied aims through constitutive features of language use is understood as an opaque process. In the therapeutic context, certain constitutive communicational behaviors are reified as "the unconscious" and are interpreted as disguised versions of embodied aims.

That is, just as "the mind" is in significant part a reification of the referential properties of language, "the unconscious" is in significant part a reification of certain of the constitutive functions of language. When I interpret the language of a patient in psychotherapy to mean that he has an unconscious desire to sleep with the mother of his childhood, what I most likely mean is that the way he uses language conveys that purpose along with other, more obvious, intentions. What are usually called the "hidden meanings," embedded in a stretch of language, meanings that are recoverable by the work of interpretation, are in the terms being used here nothing other than constitutive functions of that stretch of language, things it does. There is no need here to reify the dynamic unconscious as a place or a part of the mind.[5]

A social scientific theory of volition?

I became interested in the conversion narrative in part because it seemed to provide a paradigm of volitional behavior. Through the conversion, believers say that they are able to change what they are: such a transformation is surely what we mean when we speak of volition, the human ability to make an undetermined choice. In studying conversions, I have observed self-transformation, and I hope I have shown here what that process entails in some specific instances.

In all the instances studied, I have argued, constitutive communicative processes are brought within the realm of self by labeling them in the canonical language of Evangelical Christianity. But I have yet to provide a more general account of why such a process should work. How can it happen that language can come to label previously inarticulable experience with such genuineness that such experience can enter the realm of the referential? A slightly different way to put this question is: 'Whence the human ability to grasp metaphor?' How are people able to understand communications not on the basis of familiarity, but on some other basis? To answer this question would be at least a start on a theory of volition because it would explain something of the human ability to make up something new, to alter the boundaries of the realm of literal meaning.

I would like to suggest, however, that this is an unproductive question. It is, in essence, the same question that is answered, in the context of self-transformation, by Evangelical Christianity. The answer there is that humans may understand something new with the help of God. Social sciences, eschewing such mysticism, have offered a succession of alternative and presumably more scientific explanations: human creativity and agency can be explained by the unconscious, by the symbol, by language, by culture. But all these answers share with that offered by Christianity the claim that it is a powerful and somewhat mysterious invisible entity that in the end explains agency. In effect, social scientific theories of volition are, like religions, explanations which appropriate human agency and locate it in one or another opacity. And the effect of such explanations is just the same as that which occurs in religions: social groups are generated based on adherence to those explanations.

What is needed today in social science is a language that acknowledges the centrality of human creativity without appropriating volition to a grand theoretical construct. Some recent literature on metaphor, or on tropes in general, has come close to doing this. For example, Roy Wagner (1986) argues in a recent paper that semiotic accounts of meaning have appropriated to the sign itself the capacity of the language-user to link conventional categories to experience, and that in so doing such accounts have elided the very heart of the cultural process. The center of that process, he suggests, is based in use of tropes:

> Only the experience of "finding" or situating language's delimited in the "reading" or "hearing" of trope can give words and language itself an experiential concreteness and validity. Hence the experience of fixing analogy within the delimiting orders and relations, of having them resonate specific meanings, is the primary experience of language itself. (Ibid.: 10)

To be confronted with a trope, a figure that cannot be immediately interpreted according to the referential meanings of the words involved, is to be thrown back upon one's experience in an attempt to feel what the figure might mean. In Paul Ricoeur's (1978: 9) terms, poetic discourse reveals our "deep-seated insertion in the life world." This is as far as I want to go in the direction of explanation: there is an unspecifiable human ability both to formulate and to make sense of new language. One must be careful not to allow the tropic to become another form of opacity.

The possibility of certain sorts of language formulating something new in experience is not, in this argument, dependent upon a particular sort of marked language that is richer, "more symbolic" than other language. What canonical language shares with tropes – and with any metaphoric processes that are subjected to scrutiny – is, above all, that its use is culturally valued. One notices this language as language, and thereby looks beyond its immediate literal meaning. In concentrating on the language as language, something new may be discovered.

Rather than seeking a theory of how people produce and grasp unfamiliar language, it would be best to simply observe and study instances of such activity. One will thereby immerse oneself in the details of social processes of communication, commitment and creativity rather than turning one's attention to the grand construct that presumably accounts for these processes. Immersion in these details has two aspects. The first is the ethnographic, the study of the referential. However, the work of ethnography is never, as it has sometimes been conceived, an inquiry into the absolute limits of the imaginable in particular societies. It should instead be conceived as an investigation of, as I have put it earlier, the immediately imaginable. For the boundaries of the referential are always shifting. One can never assume a simple equivalence between the imagination and conventionalized glosses of cultural symbols.

The second aspect of a social science without a theory of volition is a study of the continual transformation of the referential through the interpretation of metaphoric processes. Human action is never merely a reflection of available cultural symbolism, however powerful a force the latter may be. Thus I argue for studies of actors formulating and making sense of new language, abilities that are richly observable once one adopts a fine focus on activity. Such study would have as its goal the replacement of opacity by rational discourse. The analyst would seek to clarify in literal terms the metaphoric practices that come into play in various aspects of social life. This seems to me a more pressing and potentially useful task than that of formulating a theory of volition.

An anthropology capable of embracing both social structure and human agency, of analyzing the role of culture in the ongoing production and reproduction of social life, must attend to the interplay of the constitutive with the referential. To focus on this dialectic is to begin to look, in a detailed and productive way, at how actors use cultural resources. It is in the fine details of that use that both the freedom and the constraint inherent to human social life may be observed.

Notes

1. The material on which this book is based was collected in the early 1980s at a location I will not disclose in order to provide the maximum protection for those who participated in the study. The project as a whole involved survey research in a population containing Evangelical Christians as well as non-believers, in-depth interviews with subjects who identified themselves as Evangelical Christians, and a short period of participant observation research at an Evangelical Christian church. Although the information gathered in all these facets of the research process undoubtedly enters, in an informal way, into my argument, this book is supported only by data gathered in the in-depth interviews.

2. Research on conversion has established that the claim to have undergone some form of self-transformation is nearly universal among converts (Snow and Machalek 1983: 264). That is, it is generally asserted that the conversion brings with it significant changes in the life of the convert: alcoholics become sober, the confused see the light, sinners become saints, and so on.

3. Recent reviews of studies of conversion are Rambo (1982), Snow and Machalek (1984), and Thumma (1991). Studies that have been of particular interest to me include James (1902), Harding (1987), Heirich (1977), Bankston, Forsyth, and Floyd (1981), Beckford (1978), Straus (1979), Whitehead (1987), Rambo (1989), Gallagher (1990), Cohen (1986), Peacock and Tyson (1989), and Peacock (1988).

4. When I say "our" society I mean American society, and more broadly "Western society." Both of these terms are of course global and vague, and are likely to embrace communities for whom any generalization is untrue. Such subtleties are peripheral to the main argument I want to advance here, however. In this book I want to discuss certain ideas about the subject that are widespread in the West, without troubling about the exact distribution of these ideas.

5. The term "reference," of course, has a number of general and specialized meanings, none of which correspond precisely to the way I want to use the term. I have chosen to use this term, in spite of these possible confusions, because of its utility for my particular purposes; "reference" can be plausibly used to designate several related phenomena whose connections I wish to explore. All that being said, it remains true that what I want to call the "referential" could be just as easily named in some other way.

6. The "referential" bias of Western culture is also discussed, in different terms from those used by Silverstein, in Wagner (1981).

7. Although the two distinctions are not the same, there are certain similarities between my formulation and one proposed by Roy Wagner (1981), who speaks of the difference between conventional and differentiating symbolizations. There may also be a distant relationship between referential and constitutive communicative behaviors and what Clifford Geertz (1964) has called the "model of" and "model for" aspects of symbolism. However, there is also a very significant difference between these terminologies. When Geertz refers to the "model for" aspect of symbolism he means to point to the way symbols may work to organize some manifestation in the physical world, as in a blueprint for a building. By "constitutive behavior" I mean to designate not the ability of the symbol to function as a model for some reality, but rather to a communicational behavior that constitutes the reality of a social situation.

It should also be noted that what I am calling constitutive functions of communication are similar to functions that are often referred to by terms such as "indexical" and "pragmatic." Although it would in some ways be preferable to adopt a pre-existing terminology, these latter terms have technical meanings in linguistics, and my use of the term "constitutive" does not correspond precisely to the accepted meanings of these terms.

8. In discussing how indexical tokens constitute situations in language, Silverstein (1976, 1979) distinguishes relatively presupposing (e.g. English this, that) from relatively creative (e.g. German Sie, Du) functions. Both of these uses of speech fit into my definition of constitutive communicative behaviors.

9. Beckford (1978) and Snow and Machalek (1984: 175ff.) also point to the problematic nature of converts' stories about themselves. More generally, the problem of the relationship between events and the narratives that ostensibly describe them is a topic that has been much discussed in recent years. See, for example, Quinn and Holland (1987: 7), Briggs (1986), and Bauman (1986: 5). I should emphasize that my point is not that the conversion event cannot be assumed to be represented in the conversion narrative, but rather that the nature of that representation is not transparent. I will assume, as I must, that the narrative is part of a genuine attempt to tell "what happened."

10. Of course, a social scientist might in fact observe her own conversion or that of someone close to her, perhaps she might even get it on videotape. She would still not have perfectly recorded the event, because the event is a symbolic construction.

2   CHARACTER AND INTENTION

1. Although aspects of American common sense are beginning to be described, particularly by cognitive scientists (see for example Quinn 1987, D'Andrade 1987), there is as far as I know no published account of what I call the "character and intention" system.

2. I do not mean to imply that Anscombe's complex treatment of intention is simply a recapitulation of Western common sense. In some respects, of course, she is concerned to investigate the use of the word in English, but her account goes well beyond the aspects of it that I have cited here in explicating the common-sense view.

3. Although some would take issue with me, I would argue that in this view the realm of intentional action is at least roughly congruent with what Max Weber called "social action." "Action is social," wrote Weber (1947: 88), "in so far as, by virtue of the subjective meaning attached to it by the acting individual (or individuals), it takes account of the behavior of others and is thereby oriented in its course." If the question "why did you do that?" applies to an act, that act has in a broad sense taken account of the behavior of others, and the answer to the question will produce that account. Thus to act intentionally is to act socially in Max Weber's sense.

4. Certain schools of thought within social science, such as ethnomethodology and sociolinguistics, have focused close attention upon tacit and other ambiguously intentional behaviors. The fact that these schools have to some extent remained outside the mainstream of research in the social sciences is testimony to the fact that much of social science has appropriated wholesale certain common-sense notions about intention and character that are at the core of a widespread ideology of individualism in Western society.

5. Admittedly, there are forms of character change which are not seen as particularly anomalous in our society. A medical student or military recruit, for example, may undergo a period of intensive training that seems to transform the person. Such transformation is, however, unlikely to be seen as involving the resolution of persisting conflicts that manifest themselves noticeably in a person's behavior. It is character change that does involve such resolution that I am centrally concerned with here.

6. There is a large body of literature that could be mentioned here. Some works that have influenced me include Shweder and Bourne (1984), Lindstrom (1990), Myers (1986), Chase (n.d.), Rorty (1976), Rosaldo (1980), Paul (1990), Bachnik (1992), Lutz (1985), White (1991), White and Kirkpatrick (1985), Hallowell (1976), La Fontaine (1985).

7. The relationship of the language I propose here to psychoanalytic theory is a complex one. Anyone who is familiar with psychoanalytic thought will understand both that I have been strongly influenced by psychoanalysis and that I deviate considerably from much of orthodox psychoanalytic theory. The reasons for this situation are perhaps best explained simply by referring to the work of Roy Schafer (1976). I regard my project as similar in a number of ways to his: to preserve some central insights of psychoanalysis in a language that is not tied to some of the philosophically and scientifically outdated aspects of Freudian theory.

8. The idea that what has often been conceived as psychic structure is better conceived as forms of activity comes from my reading of the work of Roy Schafer (especially Schafer 1976).

9. By framing the problem in these terms, I am hoping to largely transcend another intellectually debilitating aspect of this society's common sense, that being mind/body dualism.

10. Silverstein (1976) refers to this paraphrasability as based in the metasemantic property of language.

3   BOUNDARIES

1. The implications for interviewing of what I call the situated nature of social scientific research have been summarized and extensively discussed by Mishler (1986b) and Briggs (1986).

2. In the early 1980s I participated in a post-doctoral training program in the Departments of Anthropology and Psychiatry at the University of California, San Diego. As a part of this program, which was sponsored by the National Institute of Mental Health, I worked part-time for two years as a therapist in a community mental health clinic.

3. Some representative examples of such research are Bruner (1986), Charme (1989), Mishler (1986a), Miller et al. (1990), McAdams (1987, 1988), Gergen and Gergen (1983), and Peacock (1988).

4. One aspect of the transcriptions that is particularly dependent upon the judgment of the transcriber is emphasis by means other than loudness, which I have indicated with underlining. Although certain words are often emphasized over others in speech, it is very difficult to determine how that emphasis is produced in all cases. For this reason the lines between what I have indicated with underlining (emphasis), capital letters (loudness) and the colon (extended sound) are in practice often unclear.

   All transcriptions recorded here were either done by me or were checked by me after having been done by a research assistant. Because this project has been going on for several years and because the work of transcription is painstaking, I have used several different research assistants to help in transcribing. Their separate styles of hearing and recording may still be reflected in differences between different passages from different speakers, in spite of my attempts to render the transcriptions as uniform as possible.

   A final note: throughout the book I have probably erred in the direction of reproducing more of my informants' speech than is strictly necessary. This is intentional; it is part of an attempt to give my readers enough material to question my interpretations, if they wish to do so.

5. There is of course another slip here, at line 73, where Jean begins to say a word starting with an "s" sound and then immediately corrects herself to say "different." Although there is insufficient evidence to know what Jean is starting to say, my guess would be that the word she starts is "separate," since she immediately goes on to set up a phrase in which she can use that word. This sort of slip happens at several other points in the interview, although not in any of the material I use here.

6. I went over this case in detail with a psychoanalyst, and his opinion was that there was substantial evidence in the interview that Jean continues to be concerned with the issue of merger with her twin.

7. Steve Leavitt (personal communication, 1991) suggests another interpretation for my phrasing here, namely that I was irritated at Jean for not being more forthcoming.

8. Ellen Basso (personal communication, 1989) helped me with the interpretation of this passage.

9. Jean's "wash their hands" is of course a Bible reference. She is referring to

Pontius Pilate's action signifying his refusal to intercede on behalf of the condemned Jesus.

10. Such arguments have been made before, perhaps most capably by Melford Spiro. See, for example, Spiro (1984).

11. As this book was going to press, I encountered in Oatley (1992) a treatment of Freud's outlook on intention that to some extent overlaps with my own.

4   DREAMS

1. Jim has been recording his dreams in a journal for many years, and he brought this journal to the interview.

2. Ultimately Jim's "lack of power" may be best understood simply as a lack of the energy needed to motivate participation in life. Jim revealed in the interview that he has gone through several long periods of "bleakness and despair." From his description, these periods were certainly episodes of depression.

3. I owe this interpretation of separation from power in the dream to Tod Sloan (personal communication, 1989).

4. There is also the question of how accurately speech can reflect dreams even under the best conditions. See Tedlock (1987: 10) and references cited there.

5. It is interesting to note that at lines 48–49 a similar formulation is used to describe the appearance of Jim's father – another powerful figure – in a dream. Such parallels create Jim's conviction that his dreams constitute a series, a number of steps along the way to revelation.

5   MIRACLES

1. This conversion is described in Acts 26: 12–18.

2. Tod Sloan (personal communication, 1989) drew my attention to this interpretation.

3. Larry is probably referring to James 5: 13–16.

4. I have chosen not to discuss my own religious beliefs and the potential implications of those beliefs for this analysis because I do not think I can do so in a particularly helpful manner. Although I retain at least an aspiration to religious faith from a Protestant (Lutheran) upbringing, I doubt very much that my hand-wringings in this realm have much direct relevance for this analysis. Certainly a general curiosity underlies my interest in religious narratives, and certainly a general respect underlies my attempt to offer a social interpretation of religious commitment that is not completely reductionistic. That is all I will say. When believers asked me directly whether I was an Evangelical I told them I was not.

6   ROLES

1. In a psychoanalytically oriented diagnostic language, one might say that the style of the believers in this chapter is more histrionic or hysterical, while the believers described in the previous chapter have a more obsessive style. See Shapiro (1965).

2. See Banfield (1973) for a complete discussion of grammatical differences between direct and indirect speech.
3. There are four more places in the interview where George experiences some difficulty in speaking, although the difficulty is not as marked as in the examples I have discussed in the text. Two of these instances of difficulty in speaking occur within a few seconds of the passages I discuss and hence are closely associated with direct quotation. (One of these, occurring at lines 289–298, is discussed in the text.) The other two instances occur while George is directly quoting another speaker or, in one case, his own previous thoughts.
4. That the topic is changed at line 305 to the presence of attractive women in Reno is itself significant, for it illustrates George's tendency to overcome extreme anxiety by fantasizing about attractive women. There is another example of this at lines 237–240, where George suddenly changes the topic to women after having denied ever fighting with his father. Of course, the set of events surrounding George's conversion are perhaps the most striking example of this tendency.
5. George's reference to the fact that his conversion occurred at noon on the third day of praying is probably an intended parallel to the resurrection of Jesus, which is believed by Christians to have occurred on the third day after the crucifixion.

7   AGAINST A THEORY OF VOLITION

1. I read Tambiah (1968) and Dubois (1986) as at least pointing in this direction.
2. Common-sense views of the mind have been extensively described and criticized. The classic argument is Ryle (1949).
3. I am in no way following those authors (e.g. Szasz 1961) who state or imply that mental illness is nothing other than social intolerance of certain behaviors.
4. See note 2, chapter 3.
5. My rejection of the language of the dynamic unconscious as a *part* of the mind should not be taken to imply that I deny the existence of unconscious processes if by that term one simply means mental processes that take place outside of awareness. The argument of this book takes such processes – which I have called tacit processes – very much for granted. Spiro (n.d.) makes a similar argument about unconscious processes.

Bibliography

Alter, Robert, 1981, *The Art of Biblical Narrative*, New York: Basic Books.

Anscombe, G. E. M., 1963, *Intention* (second edition), Oxford: Basil Blackwell.

Athanassiou, C., 1986, A Study of the Vicissitudes of Identification in Twins, *International Journal of Psychoanalysis* 67: 327–35.

Austin, J. L., 1962, *How to Do Things with Words*, Oxford: Oxford University Press.

Bachnik, Jane M., 1992, The Two "Faces" of Self and Society in Japan, *Ethos* 20: 3–32.

Bakhtin, M. M., 1981, *The Dialogic Imagination*, Austin: University of Texas Press.

Banfield, Ann, 1973, Narrative Style and the Grammar of Direct and Indirect Speech, *Foundations of Language* 10: 1–39.

Bankston, William B., Craig J. Forsyth, and H. Hugh Floyd, Jr., 1981, Toward a General Model of the Process of Radical Conversion: An Interactionist Perspective on the Transformation of Self-Identity, *Qualitative Sociology* 4: 279–97.

Bateson, Gregory, Don D. Jackson, Jay Haley, and John Weakland, 1956, Toward a Theory of Schizophrenia, *Behavioral Science* 1: 251–64.

Bauman, Richard, 1986, *Story, Performance and Event: Contextual Studies of Oral Narrative*, Cambridge: Cambridge University Press.

Beckford, James A., 1978, Accounting for Conversion, *British Journal of Sociology* 29: 249–62.

Bellah, Robert N., 1970, Review of "Love's Body," by Norman O. Brown, in Robert N. Bellah (ed.), *Beyond Belief*, pp. 230–6, New York: Harper & Row.

Bourdieu, Pierre, 1977, *Outline of a Theory of Practice*, Cambridge: Cambridge University Press.

Briggs, Charles, 1986, *Learning How to Ask*, Cambridge: Cambridge University Press.

Bruner, Jerome, 1986, *Actual Minds, Possible Worlds*, Cambridge, Mass.: Harvard University Press.

Burke, Kenneth, 1970, *The Rhetoric of Religion* (second edition), Berkeley: University of California Press.

Caldwell, Patricia, 1983, *The Puritan Conversion Narrative: The Beginnings of American Expression*, Cambridge: Cambridge University Press.

Capps, Charles, 1976, *God's Creative Power Will Work for You*, Tulsa, Oklahoma: Harrison House.

Carrither, David W., 1985, The Defense of Insanity and Presidential Peril, *Society* 22 (5): 23–7.

Charme, Stuart L., 1989, *Meaning and Myth in the Study of Lives*, Philadelphia: University of Pennsylvania Press.

Chase, Susan, n.d., Stories of Power and Subjection: The Work Narratives of Women Educational Leaders, unpublished book manuscript, files of the author.

Cohen, Charles Lloyd, 1986, *God's Caress: The Psychology of Puritan Religious Experience*, Oxford: Oxford University Press.

Crapanzano, Vincent, 1981, Text, Transference and Indexicality, *Ethos* 9: 122–48.

Crites, Stephen, 1971, The Narrative Quality of Experience, *Journal of the American Academy of Religion* 39: 291–311.

Crocker, J. Christopher, 1977, The Social Functions of Rhetorical Forms, in D. Sapir and J. C. Crocker (eds.), *The Social Use of Metaphor*, pp. 33–66, Philadelphia: University of Pennsylvania Press.

Csordas, Thomas, 1990, Embodiment as a Paradigm for Anthropology, *Ethos* 18: 5–47.

D'Andrade, Roy, 1987, A Folk Model of the Mind, in Naomi Quinn and Dorothy Holland (eds.), *Cultural Models in Language and Thought*, pp. 112–48, Cambridge: Cambridge University Press.

1990, Some Propositions About the Relations Between Culture and Human Cognition, in James W. Stigler, Richard A. Shweder, and Gilbert Herdt (eds.), *Cultural Psychology: Essays on Comparative Human Development*, pp. 65–129, Cambridge: Cambridge University Press.

Davidson, Donald, 1984, What Metaphors Mean, in Ernest LePore (ed.), *Inquiries into Truth and Interpretation*, pp. 245–64, Oxford: Clarendon Press.

1986, A Nice Derangement of Epitaphs, in Ernest LePore (ed.), *Inquiries into Truth and Interpretation: Perspectives on the Philosophy of Donald Davidson*, pp. 433–46, Oxford: Basil Blackwell.

Devereux, George, 1967, *From Anxiety to Method in the Behavioral Sciences*, Hawthorne, N.Y.: Mouton.

Dibble, E. and D. J. Cohen, 1981, Personality Development in Identical Twins, *Psychoanalytic Study of the Child* 36: 45–70.

Douglas, Ann, 1977, *The Feminization of American Culture*, New York: Knopf.

Dubois, John W., 1986, Self Evidence and Ritual Speech, in Wallace Chafe and Johanna Nichols (eds.), *Evidentiality: The Linguistic Coding of Epistemology* (Advances in Discourse Process Series, vol. XX), pp. 313–36, Norwood, N. J.: Ablex Publishing Corporation.

Dumont, Louis, 1965, On Individualism, *Contributions to Indian Sociology* 8: 13–61.

Duranti, Alessandro and Charles Goodwin, 1992, *Rethinking Context: Language as an Interactive Phenomenon*, Cambridge: Cambridge University Press.

Erikson, Erik H., 1956, The Problem of Ego Identity, *Journal of the American Psychoanalytic Association* 4: 56–121.

Fillmore, Charles, 1982, Towards a Descriptive Framework for Spatial Deixis, in R. J. Jarvella and W. Klein (eds.), *Speech, Place, and Action*, pp. 31–59, London: John Wiley.

Freud, Sigmund, 1952, *A General Introduction to Psychoanalysis*, New York: Pocket Books.

1964, New Introductory Lectures on Psychoanalysis, in James Strachey (ed.), *The Standard Edition of the Complete Psychological Works of Sigmund Freud*, vol. XXII, London: Hogarth Press.

Gallagher, Eugene V., 1990, *Expectation and Experience: Explaining Religious Conversion*, Atlanta: Scholars Press.

Geertz, Clifford, 1964, Religion as a Cultural System, in Michael Banton (ed.), *Anthropological Approaches to the Study of Religion*, pp. 1–46, London: Tavistock.

1973, Person, Time and Conduct in Bali, in Clifford Geertz (ed.), *The Interpretation of Cultures*, pp. 360–411, New York: Basic Books.

Gergen, Kenneth J. and Mary M. Gergen, 1983, Narratives of the Self, in Theodore R. Sarbin and Karl E. Scheibe (eds.), *Studies in Social Identity*, pp. 254–73, New York: Praeger.

Gerstner, John H., 1975, The Theological Boundaries of Evangelical Faith, in David F. Wells and John D. Woodbridge (eds.), *The Evangelicals*, pp. 21–37, Nashville: Abingdon Press.

Giddens, Anthony, 1987, *Social Theory and Modern Sociology*, Stanford: Stanford University Press.

Goffman, Erving, 1981, *Forms of Talk*, Philadelphia: University of Pennsylvania Press.

1986, *Frame Analysis: An Essay on the Organization of Experience*, (first published in 1974), Boston: Northeastern University Press.

Grice, H. P., 1957, Meaning, *Philosophical Review* 66: 377–88.

Hallowell, A. Irving, 1976, Ojibwa Ontology, Behavior and World View, in A. Irving Hallowell (ed.), *Contributions to Anthropology: Selected Papers of A. Irving Hallowell*, Chicago: University of Chicago Press.

Hanks, William F., 1990, *Referential Practice: Language and Lived Space Among the Maya*, Chicago: University of Chicago Press.

Harding, Susan F., 1987, Convicted by the Holy Spirit: The Rhetoric of Fundamental Baptist Conversion, *American Ethnologist* 14: 167–81.

Heirich, Max, 1977, Change of Heart: A Test of Some Widely Held Theories about Religious Conversion, *American Journal of Sociology* 83: 653–80.

Hill, Jane, 1990, Weeping as a Meta-signal in a Mexicano Woman's Narrative, in Ellen B. Basso, (ed.), *Native Latin American Cultures Through their Discourse*, (*Journal of Folklore Research*, vol. 27, nos. 1–2).

1991, The Production of Self in Narrative. Paper read at the conference of the Society for Psychological Anthropology, Chicago.

n.d. The Voices of Don Gabriel: Responsibility and Self in a Modern Mexicano Narrative, in B. Mannheim and D. Tedlock (eds.), *Dialogical Anthropology*, Philadelphia: University of Pennsylvania Press. In Press.

Hunter, James Davison, 1983, *American Evangelicalism: Conservative Religion and the Quandary of Modernity*, New Brunswick, N.J.: Rutgers University Press.

Hymes, Dell, 1979, Sapir, Competence, Voices, in C. J. Fillmore, D. Kempler, and W. Wang (eds.), *Individual Differences in Language Ability and Language Behavior*, pp. 33–45, New York: Academic Press.

1981, Breakthrough Into Performance, in Dell Hymes (ed.), *In Vain I Tried to Tell You*, pp. 79–141, Philadelphia: University of Pennsylvania Press.

James William, 1902, *The Varieties of Religious Experience, A Study in Human Nature*, New York: Modern Library.

Kantzer, Kenneth S., 1975, Unity and Diversity in Evangelical Faith, in David Wells and John Woodbridge (eds.), pp. 38–67, *The Evangelicals*, Nashville: Abingdon Press.

La Fontaine, J. S., 1985, Person and Individual: Some Anthropological Reflections, in Michael Carrithers, Steven Collins, and Steven Lukes (eds.), *The Category of the Person*, pp. 123–40, Cambridge: Cambridge University Press.

Labov, William and David Fanshel, 1977, *Therapeutic Discourse: Psychotherapy as Conversation*, New York: Academic Press.

Lakoff, George, 1987, *Women, Fire and Dangerous Things: What Categories Reveal about the Mind*, Chicago: University of Chicago Press.

Lakoff, George and Mark Johnson, 1980, *Metaphors We Live By*, Chicago: University of Chicago Press.

Lee, Dorothy, 1950, Notes on the Conception of the Self Among the Wintu Indians, *Journal of Abnormal and Social Psychology* 45: 538–43.

Leonard, Marjorie, 1961, Identification in Twins, *The Psychoanalytic Study of the Child* 16: 300–20.

Lévi-Strauss, Claude, 1963, The Effectiveness of Symbols, in Claude Lévi-Strauss (ed.), *Structural Anthropology*, pp. 186–205, New York: Basic Books.

Lindstrom, Lamont, 1990, *Knowledge and Power in a South Pacific Society*, Washington: Smithsonian Institution Press.

Lutz, Catherine, 1985, Ethnopsychology Compared to What? Explaining Behavior and Consciousness Among the Ifaluk, in G. White and J. Kirkpatrick (eds.), *Person Self and Experience*, pp. 35–79, Berkeley, University of California Press.

McAdams, Dan P., 1987, A Life Story Model of Identity, *Perspectives in Psychology* 2: 15–50.

 1988, Biography, Narrative, and Lives: An Introduction, *Journal of Personality* 56: 1–18.

Mahler, Margaret, Fred Pine, and A. Bergman, 1975, *The Psychological Birth of the Human Infant*, New York: Basic Books.

Malinowski, Bronislaw, 1954, *Magic, Science and Religion and Other Essays*, Garden City, N.Y.: Douleday Anchor Books.

Mauss, Marcel, 1985, A Category of the Human Mind: The Notion of Person; The Notion of Self, in M. Carrithers, S. Collins, and S. Lukes (eds.), *The Category of the Person*, pp. 1–25, Cambridge: Cambridge University Press.

Merton, Robert, 1968, *Social Theory and Social Structure* (1968 enlarged edition), New York: Free Press.

Miller, Peggy J., Randolph Potts, Heidi Fung, Lisa Hoogstra, and Judy Mintz, 1990, Narrative Practices and the Social Construction of Self in Childhood, *American Ethnologist* 17: 292–311.

Mishler, Elliot G., 1986a, The Analysis of Interview Narratives, in Theodore R. Sarbin (ed.), *Narrative Psychology: The Storied Nature of Human Conduct*, pp. 233–55, New York: Praeger.

 1986b, *Research Interviewing: Context and Narrative*, Cambridge, Mass.: Harvard University Press.

1991, Representing Discourse: The Rhetoric of Transcription, *Journal of Narrative and Life History*, 1: 255-80.

Moerman, Michael, 1988, *Talking Culture: Ethnography and Conversation Analysis*, Philadelphia: University of Pennsylvania Press.

Myers, Fred, 1979, Emotions and the Self: A Theory of Personhood and Political Order among the Pintupi Aborigines, *Ethos* 7: 343–70.

1986, *Pintupi Country, Pintupi Self: Sentiment, Place, and Politics Among Western Desert Aborigines*, Washington: Smithsonian Institution Press.

Needham, Rodney, 1972, *Belief, Language and Experience*, Chicago: University of Chicago Press.

Oatley, Keith, 1992, *Best Laid Schemes: The Psychology of Emotions*, Cambridge: Cambridge University Press.

Obeyesekere, Gananath, 1981, *Medusa's Hair: An Essay on Personal Symbols and Religious Experience*, Chicago: University of Chicago Press.

Ochs, Elinor, 1979. Transcription as Theory, in Elinor Ochs and Bambi B. Schieffelin (eds.), *Developmental Pragmatics*, pp. 43–72, London: Academic Press.

Paul, Robert A., 1990, Act and Intention in Sherpa Culture and Society, unpublished paper, files of the author.

Peacock, James L., 1988, Religion and Life History: An Exploration in Cultural Psychology, in Edward M. Bruner (ed.), *Text, Play and Story*, pp. 94–116, Prospect Heights, Ill.: Waveland Press.

Peacock, James L. and Ruel W. Tyson, Jr., 1989, *Pilgrims of Paradox: Calvinism and Experience among the Primitive Baptists of the Blue Ridge*, Washington: Smithsonian Institution Press.

Peirce, Charles Sanders, 1932, *Collected Papers of Charles Sanders Peirce*, Cambridge, Mass.: Harvard University Press.

Pinson, Koppel S., 1934, *Pietism as a Factor in the Rise of German Nationalism*, New York: Columbia University Press.

Polanyi, Michael, 1962, *Personal Knowledge: Towards a Post-Critical Philosophy*, Chicago: University of Chicago Press.

Polkinghorne, Donald E., 1988, *Narrative Knowing and the Human Sciences*, Albany: State University of New York Press.

Popper, Karl R., 1957, *The Poverty of Historicism*, New York: Harper Torchbooks.

Quine, W. V., 1979, A Postscript on Metaphor, in Sheldon Sacks (ed.), *On Metaphor*, pp. 159–60, Chicago: University of Chicago Press.

Quinn, Naomi, 1987, Convergent Evidence for a Cultural Model of American Marriage, in Naomi Quinn and Dorothy Holland (eds.), *Cultural Models in Language and Thought*, pp. 173–92, Cambridge: Cambridge University Press.

Quinn, Naomi and Dorothy Holland, 1987, Culture and Cognition, in Naomi Quinn and Dorothy Holland (eds.), *Cultural Models in Language and Thought*, pp. 3–40, Cambridge: Cambridge University Press.

Rambo, Lewis, 1982, Current Research on Religious Conversion, *Religious Studies Review* 8: 146–59.

1989, Conversion: Toward a Holistic Model of Religious Change, *Pastoral Psychology* 38: 47–63.

Rappaport, Roy, 1977, The Obvious Aspects of Ritual, in Roy Rappaport (ed.), *Ecology, Meaning and Religion*, pp. 173–221, Richmond, Calif.: North Atlantic Books.

Ricoeur, Paul, 1978, Imagination in Discourse and Action, *Analecta Husserliana* 7 (3): 3–22.

Rorty, Amelie Oksenberg, 1976, A Literary Postscript: Characters, Persons, Selves, Individuals, in Amelie Rorty (ed.), *The Identities of Persons*, pp. 301–23, Berkeley: University of California Press.

Rorty, Richard, 1987, Hesse and Davidson on Metaphor, *Aristotelian Society Supplement* 61: 283–96.

1989, The Contingency of Language, in Richard Rorty (ed.), *Contingency, Irony and Solidarity*, pp. 3–22, Cambridge: Cambridge University Press.

1991, Non-reductive Physicalism, in Richard Rorty (ed.), *Objectivity, Relativism and Truth. Philosophical Papers*, vol. I, pp. 113–25, Cambridge: Cambridge University Press.

Rosaldo, Michelle Z., 1980, *Knowledge and Passion: Ilongot Notions of Self and Social Life*, Cambridge: Cambridge University Press.

Rosch, Eleanor, 1975, Cognitive Reference Points, *Cognitive Psychology* 7: 532–47.

Rosch, Eleanor and Carolyn Mervis, 1975, Family Resemblances: Studies in the Internal Structure of Categories, *Cognitive Psychology* 7: 573–605.

Rumsey, Alan, 1990, Wording, Meaning and Linguistic Ideology, *American Anthropologist* 92: 346–61.

Ryle, Gilbert, 1949, *The Concept of Mind*, New York: Barnes & Noble.

Sacks, H., E. Schegloff, and G. Jefferson, 1974, A Simplest Semantics for the Organization for Turn-Taking for Conversations, *Language* 50: 696–735.

Schafer, Roy, 1976, *A New Language for Psychoanalysis*, New Haven: Yale University Press.

Schieffelin, Edward L., 1985, Performance and the Cultural Construction of Reality, *American Ethnologist* 12: 707–24.

Shapiro, David, 1965, *Neurotic Styles*, New York: Basic Books.

1981, *Autonomy and Rigid Character*, New York: Basic Books.

Shweder, Richard and Edmund J. Bourne, 1984, Does the Concept of the Person Vary Cross-Culturally? in Richard A. Shweder and Robert A. Levine (eds.), *Culture Theory*, pp. 158–99, Cambridge: Cambridge University Press.

Silverstein, Michael, 1976, Shifters, Linguistic Categories, and Cultural Description, in K. Basso and H. A. Selby (eds.), *Meaning in Anthropology*, pp. 11–55, Albuquerque: University of New Mexico Press.

1979, Language Structure and Linguistic Ideology, in P. R. Clyne, W. Hanks, and C. Hoffbrauer (eds.), *The Elements: A Parasession on Linguistic Units and Levels*, pp. 193–248, Chicago: Chicago Linguistic Society.

Simon, Rita J. and David E. Aaronson, 1988, *The Insanity Defense: A Critical Assessment of Law and Policy in the Post-Hinckley Era*, New York: Praeger.

Snow, David A. and Richard Machalek, 1983, The Convert as a Social Type, in R. Collins (ed.), *Sociological Theory*, pp. 259–89, San Francisco: Jossey-Bass.

1984, The Sociology of Conversion, *Annual Review of Sociology* 10: 167–90.

Spiro, Melford, 1965, Religious Systems as Culturally Constituted Defense

Mechanisms, in Melford Spiro (ed.), *Context and Meaning in Cultural Anthropology*, pp. 100–13, New York: The Free Press.

1984, Some Reflections on Family and Religion in East Asia, in George Devos and Takao Sofue (eds.), *Religion and Family in East Asia*, pp. 35–54, Osaka, Japan: National Museum of Ethnology, *Senri Ethnological Studies 11*.

n.d., Tropes, Defenses, and Unconscious Mental Representations: Some Critical Reflections on the Primary Process, *Psychoanalysis and Contemporary Thought*. In Press.

Stoeffler, F. Ernest, 1965, *German Pietism during the Eighteenth Century*, Leiden: E. J. Brill.

Straus, Roger A., 1979, Religious Conversion as a Personal and Collective Accomplishment, *Sociological Analysis* 40 (2): 158–65.

Stromberg, Peter G., 1986, *Symbols of Community*, Tucson: University of Arizona Press.

Szasz, Thomas, 1961, *The Myth of Mental Illness*, New York: Hoeber-Harper.

Tambiah, Stanley J., 1968, The Magical Power of Words, *Man* 3: 175–208.

1988, A Performative Approach to Ritual, in Stanley J. Tambiah (ed.), *Culture, Thought and Social Action*, pp. 123–66, Cambridge, Mass.: Harvard University Press.

Tedlock, Barbara, 1987, Dreaming and Dream Research, in Barbara Tedlock (ed.), *Dreaming: Anthropological and Psychological Interpretations*, pp. 1–30, Cambridge: Cambridge University Press.

Thumma, Scott, 1991, Seeking to be Converted: An Examination of Recent Conversion Studies and Theories, *Pastoral Psychology* 39: 185–94.

Urban, Greg, 1989, The "I" of Discourse, in Benjamin Lee and Greg Urban (eds.), *Semiotics, Self and Society*, pp. 27–51, New York: Mouton de Gruyter.

Varenne, Herve, n.d., Ambiguous Harmony, unpublished book manuscript, files of the author.

Volosinov, V. N., 1973, *Marxism and the Philosophy of Language*, New York: Seminar Press.

Wagner, Roy, 1981, *The Invention of Culture* (revised and expanded edition), Chicago: University of Chicago Press.

1986, Imaginary Competence. Paper read at the 85th annual meeting of the American Anthropological Association.

Wallace, Anthony F. C., 1970, *The Death and Rebirth of the Seneca*, New York: Alfred A. Knopf.

Weber, Max, 1947, *The Theory of Social and Economic Organization*, New York: The Free Press.

White, Geoffrey, M., 1991, *Identity Through History: Living Stories in a Solomon Islands Society*, Cambridge: Cambridge University Press.

White, Geoffrey M. and John Kirkpatrick, 1985, *Person, Self and Experience: Exploring Pacific Ethnopsychologies*, Berkeley: University of California Press.

Whitehead, Harriet, 1987, *Renunciation and Reformulation: A Study of Conversion in an American Sect*, Ithaca: Cornell University Press.

Index

S